THE BEST
GRILLING
COOKBOOK

Ever Written by Two Idiots

RYAN FEY   *The Grill Dads*   MARK ANDERSON

PAGE STREET
PUBLISHING CO.

PAGE STREET
PUBLISHING CO.

First published in 2022 by
Page Street Publishing Co.
27 Congress Street, Suite 1511
Salem, MA 01970
www.pagestreetpublishing.com

Distributed by Macmillan, sales in Canada by The Canadian Manda Group.

26 25 24 23 22   2 3 4 5

ISBN-13: 978-1-64567-606-5
ISBN-10: 1-64567-606-4

Library of Congress Control Number: 2021952283

Cover design by Amy Wilk. Book design by Emma Hardy for Page Street Publishing Co. Photography by Ken Goodman. Photography on the top of page 7 by Michelle Bliss. Food styling by Amanda Hood.

Printed and bound in the United States of America

THE DADS' DEDICATION

We'd like to dedicate this book to our friends and family, who have supported us, and put up with our shit, during our crazy culinary journey. But we'd also like to dedicate this book to you, the person reading it. We believe great food is for everyone, and that you don't have to be a professional to create an awesome culinary experience for your loved ones. So we hope you will find our recipes not only delicious, but fun and easy to make.
Thank you for supporting us.

TABLE OF
CONTENTS

Foreword

I met Mark and Fey on a commercial set that I was directing for their ad agency. I quickly realized we were food soul mates as we never spoke about the project or camera shots, but instead obsessed over recipes and spices. (Hence why the commercial never made the air.) They gifted me with their lovely spice line from Spiceology where they expertly crafted the perfect balance of flavor and heat in each bottle. My Ancho Chili–Rubbed Skirt Steak Tacos (page 45) have never been the same since the Red Tuxedo spice mix, and I won't dare make poultry without their brilliant dry brine called Lemonade Thyme. Only these two knuckleheads figured out that meat would benefit from a one-two punch of Mexican chocolate and activated charcoal.

I was lucky enough to be a guest on their podcast where we talked about all things food, but mostly about grilling. I'm from Texas where grilling is a pre-requisite to cooking. I was blown away at the fearless approach these guys had towards throwing it all on the grill. From the traditional bone-in Ribeye to Jalapeño Popper Stuffed Pork Tenderloin (page 80) to Grilled, Grilled Cheese (page 138). Their Instagram page is full of surprises and innovation, and offers so much to those anxiously waiting with tongs in their hands.

So many people are intimidated by the grill. They only pull off the cover for the 4th of July BBQ or that occasional Superbowl party (then mostly avoid their grill because they don't want to clean it). But other than that, it's a tool that often sits idle on your back porch. This book will empower you to light up that grill and use it to its full potential. After meeting these guys, I have hardly gone back to my oven! (Oven, what oven?) From grilled cauliflower to Smoky Chicken Noodle Soup (page 69), there is nothing your grill can't handle.

The boys and I agree on a lot of things. Firstly, steakhouses suck and you can ALWAYS make a better steak at home! I strongly feel this way about roasted chicken as well. Why go to a restaurant and order a $30 dry chicken when you can grill one up at home that tastes way better with Mark and Fey's guide to poultry? There's nothing these guys won't cook on the grill, including donut ice cream sandwiches (page 191)! Their intelligence and wit comes through in each recipe and technique. So next time you're standing in front of that hunk of steel, arm yourself with this book.

You have never read a grilling cookbook like this one. No one can compare to The Grill Dads!

Grill away!

—Eva Longoria Baston, actor, director, producer and wannabe chef

A Note
From Our Kids

My favorite food in the world is probably the strawberry French toast that Daddy makes and is in this cookbook (page 157). There's other food in here that I really like and you probably will, too. Also remember that most of the food in here is grilled, so you will need a grill. My favorite grills are the Big Green Egg®, the pellet grill and the gas grill. So . . . start grilling!

—Arthur Anderson (Mark's son, age 7)

Hi. I'm Zoe—Fey's daughter. And I love to cook, especially with my dad and Uncle Momo (Mark). Because first off, he is a Grill Dad and I love him, but I also love how much fun it is to create new things and make your own masterpieces! And you don't have to go buy some stupid cookbook to make great food (oh wait, that's what this is . . . my bad, Dad. Love you). What I mean is, you can add your own twist to things and express yourself by cooking fantastic meals. Everybody wins! So just have fun with this book! It does not matter if you are vegan, vegetarian, omnivore (me), pollotarian, pescatarian or a carnivore. Have fun cooking with your family and friends, and enjoy this book! I approve this message.

—Zoe Fey (Fey's daughter, age 13)

Hi,

We're Mark and Fey, and yes, we're the two idiots.

So why did we decide to refer to ourselves as idiots on the cover of our first published book, which is being internationally distributed and potentially read by our moms?

Whether we're making a TV show for the Food Network, cooking on *The Today Show*, working with big brands or writing a book, *we've always strived to make elevated grilling at home fun and attainable*. We have always joked that people at home watch us and say, "If these two idiots can do it, I can." And, oddly enough, this brings us great joy.

We aren't trained chefs; in fact, we have never cooked professionally. We never attended culinary school. Nope. We're just like you. Home chefs. Backyard connoisseurs. Grill enthusiasts. Weekend warriors.

Grilling and barbecue are different. See, grills are a tool, a versatile heat source. BBQ, on the other hand, is a cuisine. And we are not guys who concentrate on making great low-and-slow BBQ—although we do enjoy doing that from time to time.

We focus on showing people how to use grills to cook anything and everything. From soups and salads to mains and appetizers—the grill is the most multifaceted tool we've ever used to turn out inventive and delicious food with a kiss of smoke and fire.

It's with this idea that we are incredibly proud to introduce you to this cookbook as a way to express yourself and experiment with different types of grills, cooking methods and cuisines—with recipes designed to help you grow as the home chef you want to be. We've worked hard to create simple, fun and delicious recipes that you can follow as written, or use as a guide to make each one your own. We've provided the road map and now you can take the journey. This book was written for everyone—not just those folks who wear "Kiss the Chef" aprons and sport New Balance sneakers reserved only for mowing the grass. This is for the modern dads, moms and families who want to use the glory of the grill to turn out delicious and inventive dishes everyone will enjoy.

We're excited to show you how to use a variety of techniques and different types of grills designed to put a unique spin on some of your favorite flavors and dishes.

Read This First
(Which Is Why We Put It Up Front)

MEET THE GRILLS

We aren't grill snobs. We use pellet grills, gas grills and charcoal grills. There are more, like offset stick burner smokers and griddles, but we are going to focus on the big three here.

Every type has perks and trade-offs. We get daily requests for grill recommendations, and we always ask people about their budget and their three favorite things to cook outside.

PELLET GRILLS

Pellet grills are known for their ease of use and great low-and-slow capabilities. They are the set-it-and-forget-it of barbecue. It really feels like the 21st century when your grill sends you a text message letting you know your brisket is almost done.

Pros: Precise temperature control, app connectivity, consistent and even cooking, easy and fast to light and easy to clean.

Cons: They have a hard time maintaining a temperature in cold or windy conditions, and they don't have great high-heat cooking capabilities.

Things to cook in them: We like to use this grill for dishes cooked in the 200°F (95°C) to 400°F (205°C) range. Barbecue (ribs, pork shoulder, beef ribs, brisket), beer-can chicken, turkey, seafood, enchiladas, pies, frittata, wings, potatoes . . .

Price: $200 to $5,000. The higher prices get you wider temperature ranges and better insulation, which allows you to cook evenly and efficiently. It also costs a bit more to get into the bells and whistles with app integration.

GAS GRILLS

Gas grills can get you where you want to go, quickly. Spring for natural gas if you can swing it. Nobody likes to run to the store for a propane swap mid-cook.

Pros: Easy to light, quickly gets to temperature, has great high-temperature range, easy to clean and cooks great with the lid open.

Cons: No smoke/wood/charcoal flavor (which can be remedied with accessories), and it doesn't perform well at low temperatures.

Things to cook in them: Burgers, dogs, pizza, steak, chicken, casseroles, veggies and potatoes.

Price: $100 to $15,000. The differences driving price are quality of material, cooking surface area, number of burners and additional features such as sear burners, a rotisserie and side burners. If you spend much less than $350, expect the grill to last 1 to 2 years as the burners and heat deflectors will break down quickly.

If you'd like to turn your gas grill into a smoker, you have a few options. You can buy a super reasonable smoker box on the internets. Soak some chips in water for an hour, put them in the box, then put the box right over the direct heat. Additionally, you could wrap the chips in foil and poke a few small holes in it.

CHARCOAL GRILLS

This is a broad category with lots of players. For this book we are referring to anything that burns charcoal and has a lid. We learned to grill on a kettle grill with charcoal briquettes and now we use a Big Green Egg kamado with lump hardwood charcoal. Techniques and results may be similar, but the ceramic grills, like the Big Green Egg, are more efficient and have more range. Make sure you experiment with opening and closing the top vents to get good at controlling the temperature of the grill.

Pros: Perform well from low to very high temperatures, work as a smoker and grill, great charcoal flavor and are extremely versatile.

Cons: Takes longer to come up to temperature, harder to clean and takes forever to cool down.

Things to cook in them: Anything and everything from a smoked turkey to a steak seared at 550°F (290°C) to Neapolitan pizza cooked at 750°F (400°C).

Budget: $75 to $6,000. The more expensive grills are better insulated (like ceramic) and have more cooking area.

You might be wondering how to regulate the heat when using a charcoal grill. Right? Oh, come on, it's OK that you don't know everything. Because if you did . . . you'd be us. And OK, so: The best way to regulate a charcoal grill is to understand how the air moves inside the grill. Remember, when using charcoal, you need to let in some oxygen to keep the flames burning (remember blowing on some wood as a kid to see it light up red? Same thing here). In this case, you want airflow to occur from the top and the bottom of the grill. Almost all charcoal grills have vents on the top and bottom. These can serve as dampers to either increase or decrease airflow. The more air you let into the grill, the hotter it will become. On the flip side, the less air you let into the grill from the top or bottom, the lower the temperature of the grill will be. Experiment to see how your vents impact the temperature.

TWO-ZONE, DIRECT AND INDIRECT COOKING

In this book you will see that recipes call for one of three different grill setups. They are direct, indirect and two-zone cooking. We want you to be inspired to use whatever grill you have so these recipes can all be cooked on a pellet, gas or charcoal grill. Some grills may have a certain advantage for a certain recipe, or we may prefer a different type, but they can all be done on whatever grill you have.

Direct cooking: Direct cooking is cooking food directly over the fire with high heat. For a gas grill, you would cook directly over a burner that is on. For a charcoal grill, you would cook directly over hot, white charcoal. For a pellet grill, this setup is a bit more challenging. More and more pellet grills now make it easy to remove the heat deflector and cook directly over the fire pot for direct cooking. If yours doesn't, get the cooking rack as low as possible so the food is as close to the firepot as possible.

Indirect cooking: Indirect cooking is cooking away from the fire source, for a slower, even cooking process. To set this up on a gas grill, turn half of the burners off and place the food over the burners that are off. When we cook a turkey on a gas grill, we leave the two outside burners on and the two inside burners off. For charcoal, place all your charcoal on one side of the grill and cook the food away from the charcoal. For a kamado grill, you can also use accessories like heat deflectors to get the entire grill set up for indirect. Most pellet grills' natural cooking setup is indirect. If yours isn't, you can place a pan or cooking stone on the rack below your food to help diffuse the heat.

Two-zone cooking: Quite simply, two-zone cooking is setting up a grill with heat (charcoal, gas) on one half of the grill and not the other. The heated side (direct) can be used for searing, while the unheated side (indirect) cooks more like an oven. For gas and charcoal grills, the setup is the same as indirect, but you make use of both sides of the grill while cooking. For a pellet grill, you will set it up like you would for direct cooking by removing the heat deflector for direct and using the lower, outside corners away from the fire pot for indirect.

GRILLING VERSUS SMOKING

Ah, grilling versus smoking. It's actually quite simple in terms of defining the difference between these two techniques. They can both be accomplished on the same type of grill, regardless of the fuel used. It's really all about the cooking temperature and what type of dish you are making.

The scientific differentiation between smoking and grilling is based on temperature. When a fire is burning at a lower temperature, the combustion gives off smoke (hence "smoking"). If you've ever tried to put a campfire out with a bucket of water, you know that it starts smoking as soon as the water hits the fire and cools it down. The temperature range for smoking, depending on the fuel source and grill/smoker, is 185°F (85°C) to 275°F (135°C). Hotter fires burn clean or with no smoke. Grilling is anything from 300°F (150°C) and up.

Smoking is mostly used for larger cuts of meat that require a steady, "low-and-slow" temperature and time to break down the protein and connective tissue over hours of constant heat. It can also be used to add smoke flavor to food that you don't want to expose to high heat, like salmon. It's one of the oldest forms of cooking and has been used for centuries throughout the world.

Grilling, on the other hand, is typically associated with high heat and faster cooking times, creating a type of "char" that gives the food a distinct flavor profile—one that is primal and has been used for centuries as well. Grilling also can designate that the food is touched by actual flame at some point.

We often use both techniques when cooking larger items, like thick-cut steaks, roasts and whole poultry. We will cook the protein slowly and evenly in a smoker, then grill it at high heat at the end of the cook to sear the exterior.

OTHER GRILLING TOOLS WE LOVE AND YOU NEED

A carbon steel or cast-iron pan: One of our favorite grilling tools has *nothing* to do with a grill. In fact, it's typically a tool that's used in the kitchen either on the stovetop or in the oven. Once you open your mind to using oven-safe cookware outside, the limits of grilling are endless.

Many people ask, "Why in the hell would you use a pan on a grill when you are looking to get grill marks on the food you are cooking?" Well, we have a few things to say to that:

1. Grill marks are for posers (more on that later).

2. Searing things in fat in a pan can create the perfect crust.

3. You can avoid making your house smell like smoke and grease while your significant other yells at you for triggering the smoke detectors, again.

4. A pan allows you to cook things on that grill that would normally fall into the flames—like chili, pasta, eggs, pancakes and even soup—all while imparting a delicious charcoal flavor.

A good set of spatulas and a flat-top cooking surface: These tools make amazing smashburgers like our Pinkies Up Smashburger on page 137 and one hell of a breakfast (give our Apple Pie Pancake a try on page 165). More on that in some of the upcoming recipes.

A meat thermometer: Would you ever do math without a calculator? Yeah, us neither. That's why we *always* use a meat thermometer when grilling. This will help ensure that you create perfect dishes every time. We love to use the Meater+® thermometer because it not only will tell you the temp inside the meat you are cooking, but it also uses the ambient temperature of the grill to help calculate cook time and carryover cooking.

SALT AND SEASONING

Unlike humans, all salts are not created equal. Different types of salt have different shapes, salinity and ability to dissolve.

A steak could be under-seasoned because you used a rock salt that didn't dissolve and get absorbed into the meat, falling off into the grill during cooking. Or your chicken might taste like a saltlick because you used iodized table salt instead of kosher salt. Did you know that the kosher salt used in most restaurants has only 25 percent of the salinity of table salt?

You will notice that in most cases we don't give exact amounts of salt. This is because we don't measure it. And because ingredients vary substantially in shape and size, we'd probably get salt amounts wrong. So, we salt by feel—and we think you should, too. Make sure you use the same salt, experiment with different amounts of salt and take good notes. We recommend a super mild kosher salt (the mildness can be forgiving). Before long, you will be the Salt Bae of whatever town you live in. Just please don't let it roll down your arm. That has officially jumped the shark.

Home cooks often ask us why the food they make at home doesn't taste as good as it does in restaurants. The key is seasoning. When, and how much. Here are our rules:

Iodized table salt: Use this for salting your pasta water . . . *only!*

Pre-season: We always season the food in advance. You will see that often we season protein well in advance of cooking. We use kosher salt for both pre-seasoning and seasoning on the fly. It's mild and dissolves fast. In this book we never use table salt. If a recipe doesn't clarify the type of salt, use kosher salt.

Season as you go: You want every layer of food to be seasoned individually. For example, if you are sautéing onions to add to a dish, add salt and pepper so the onions are seasoned perfectly, and can stand on their own. Typically, we use kosher salt for this as well.

Season at the end: This is the step most home cooks miss. Restaurant chefs never miss it. Seasoning at the end of cooking will awaken flavors and even add texture. For this, we like to use finishing salt, such as a mild flaky salt, but kosher salt is great, too.

Also, we have our own spice line that we developed with Spiceology. You can purchase these on Amazon and at www.thegrilldads.com. They taste great and are ready to go, but we've included spice amounts in the recipes for people that don't own our spices (yet).

WHY YOU DRY BRINE 90% OF THE TIME

Dry brining is the process of seasoning your protein with salt and other spices well in advance of cooking. For our recipes you will see 24- to 48-hour dry brines. But the world of dry brining is getting even more adventurous: There are recipes calling for 72 hours on large cuts like prime rib.

The brining process allows the seasoning to penetrate and distribute evenly throughout the meat. The salt also breaks down (aka denatures) the proteins. This keeps the proteins from constricting and squeezing juice out of the meat while cooking.

The result? Tender and perfectly seasoned meat. And with poultry, it helps create crispy skin.

Also, dry brining is way less messy than its outdated counterpart, the wet brine. Who wants to deal with a bunch of nasty water-brined turkey and figure out how to dispose of the liquid once brined? Yeah, us neither.

FRYING ON THE GRILL

We claim that you can cook anything on a grill, including fried foods. However, there are some serious inherent dangers when you fry on a grill. Follow these tips:

1. Use a taller pan than you need. You want to make sure that oil doesn't spill over into the grill and start a fire when you add the food.

2. Always pat food dry—water causes oil to spatter.

3. Don't leave the frying setup unattended, especially with children or Fey present.

4. Have a fire extinguisher nearby that is rated for oil fires.

5. Have a beer on hand in case everything goes fine and you get thirsty while you are watching your food cook perfectly.

STEAKHOUSES SUCK

MAKE A BETTER STEAK

At Home

Do steakhouses really suck? A lot of them do, at least when you're talking about the steak. They are way overpriced and oftentimes underwhelming. The sides are usually baller and the service is great, but if we want a great steak we have to make it at home.

There are three key things to consider when making a steak: the quality of the meat, the seasoning and cooking it properly. You need to nail all three of these.

When looking to activate steak god status at home, and put overpriced steakhouses in your rearview mirror, choosing your weapon is the critical first step. A great man once said, "You can't out-cook a shitty piece of meat." Well, we might be able to because we're super, super talented. But it isn't worth the risk.

Steak Basics for Ballers
Make No Misteaks

WHAT CUT WORKS FOR YOU

There are probably more than 30 different cuts of steak out there. At the end of the day, it comes down to preference. Typically, you are going to look at marbling, tenderness, flavor and price. Marbling, or fat content, is where you get a richness and flavor boost.

Here are some of our favorite steaks:

Picanha/coulotte/sirloin cap: This is the iconic Brazilian churrascaria meat on a sword. The fat cap is pronounced and melts like butter. The steak is marbled and tender, and features a sweet sirloin flavor. We cook this like a roast!

Hanger: There is only one of these per cow. It used to be an afterthought, but now its compact size, tenderness and huge flavor have it in high demand. We cook these direct.

Skirt: There are two different types of skirt steak. Inside skirt and outside skirt. You'll want to stick with the outside skirt, which is more tender, uniform and flavorful. If the package just says "skirt steak" assume the worst and walk away. We cook these direct on high heat.

Tri-tip: This West Coast staple cooks like a roast and eats like a steak. The perfect meal for a family and an ideal candidate for a reverse sear.

Flank: This lean steak has a robust flavor and a pronounced grain. Make sure you cut against the grain for a tender experience. Grill this one over direct heat!

Bavette: Aka flap meat. This comes from the bottom sirloin, and has some taste and texture similarities to outside skirt steak. We cook this direct or with a reverse sear.

Flat iron: This steak has great marbling and is very tender. We cook these hot and fast on direct heat.

T-bone/porterhouse: These steaks are a filet and a strip separated by the T-shaped bone. The difference is in the diameter of the filet. Anything over 2 inches (5 cm) is considered a porterhouse. Reverse sear for both!

Porterhouse (left) and T-Bone (right)

Strip steak: The strip is perfect for those looking for a big-personality steak but aren't quite up for the ribeye. It has great marbling and is super tender. You can use almost every method to cook this.

Petite tender or teres major: This steak is one of the most tender on the animal. Combine this with a chuck primal flavor and you have a winning combo. We cook this direct.

Ribeye: This well-marbled, classic indulgence can vary greatly depending on whether it comes from the loin end or chuck end of the rib rack. We like ours from the loin end as it has less connective tissue. The ribeye also features the cap, or spinalis, and is widely considered the best part of the animal. Some butchers will actually sell steaks that are just the cap. If you see it . . . get it. Cooking technique will vary greatly depending on the size of the steak.

Filet mignon: This steak is lean, yet tender and flavorful. The flavor is understated yet refined. You cook this with the steakhouse method (more on that on page 21) or pan sear it.

Sirloin: The sirloin is lean and juicy with a classic, nostalgic flavor profile. You can cook a sirloin over direct heat or reverse sear it.

Top round (London broil): Because of how lean it is, this steak needs some help with a marinade to get going. But it is worth the effort. Cook with a high, direct heat.

Chuck steak: This has great marbling and a classic steak flavor, but it is a heavily worked muscle with connective tissue that results in a tougher steak. We leave the chuck for pot roast.

DRY VERSUS WET AGING

Steak needs some aging for tenderness and flavor. There are all sorts of processes like enzyme breakdown and other science-y stuff that need to happen before the steak is truly enjoyable.

Wet aging happens with the steak's own juices in a vacuum-sealed package. Unless a steak says otherwise, it is a wet-aged steak.

Dry-aged beef is aged in an open cooler that encourages evaporation. This moisture loss results in a steak that has a more concentrated flavor. Additionally, mold and yeasts in the air will react and grow on the outside of the meat and develop a flavor profile similar to salami and cheese. This taste can be nutty with a bit of blue cheese funk. Because of this, the location of the dry-aging process has a big impact on the final flavor. The other major factor is the length of time that it is aged. We love a 21-day dry age because it still tastes like a familiar steak, but it has a richer and more complex flavor profile. Once you get into 45-, 60- and 90-day dry-aged steaks, the flavor makes a dramatic change. It's a bit too much funk for us, but we can certainly appreciate it.

HOW TO SELECT THE RIGHT STEAK

Steak quality is mostly judged based on the amount of intramuscular fat and how evenly it is distributed. You are looking for a lot of fat, but it should be thin ribbons of fat, not chunks.

The best way to size them all up is the Beef Marbling Score or BMS. The scale runs from 1 to 12.

USDA Select: BMS 0–1

USDA Choice: BMS 2–3

USDA Prime: BMS 4–5

American Wagyu: BMS 6–10

A5 Wagyu: BMS 8–12

Our favorite is American Wagyu. It is a cross-breed between a Japanese Wagyu cow and American Angus. The steak is more marbled than USDA Prime, but it has a familiar flavor and mouthfeel. The A5 is a fun treat, but it is too expensive and too rich to have regularly.

Be careful with Choice as the range between 2 and 3 BMS is huge. There are great Choice cuts and terrible Choice cuts. Some meat markets now offer "upper third choice," which is typically a great quality.

We roll with a Prime steak when we are looking for that classic but luxurious domestic steak.

HOW TO SEASON STEAK

People frequently ask us why a steak at home isn't as good as one at a restaurant. There are many factors, including the quality of the meat. But there is one thing most restaurants do that people at home don't do: Season the steak before it is cooked *and* after.

Start by liberally coating the meat before it is cooked with a mild kosher salt. Allow it to dissolve into the meat.

NY Strips (top to bottom): Choice, Prime, American Wagyu and A5 Wagyu

We always finish a steak with at least salt and some fat, typically olive oil, butter or some fancy sauce. This is the difference. Slice the steak and try a piece to check for seasoning. This is the time to break out the fancy flaky salt.

HOW TO COOK STEAK

Regardless of which way you choose to cook your steak, know this: Grill marks are for posers, Sizzler commercials and ridiculous steak cooking competitions. You won't see grill marks at the best and most respected restaurants in the world. Yup, we said it. And we're fucking right about this.

When you sear a steak, it causes what's known as the Maillard reaction. The high heat causes the proteins and sugars on the outside of the steak to brown and chemically react, causing browning and a flavor explosion. It adds a layer of caramelization and texture that brings out all the best parts of the steak. If you end up with grill marks you are only getting the Maillard reaction where the grill marks are located, which means you are leaving major flavor on the table.

Our Three Favorite Ways to Cook a Steak

Reverse sear: This method is perfect for larger steaks and roasts. The reverse sear means that the steak gets seared at the end. The steak is cooked at a low heat, usually 225 to 300°F (110 to 150°C) until it is almost completely cooked. Then, to develop the iconic Maillard reaction, you sear the steak over a very high direct heat or in a ripping-hot pan.

Direct: Cooking directly over the flame or coals is great for thinner steaks like skirt and flank. You've been told to only flip a steak once. You were given bad info. To allow a steak to cook evenly, flip it often. When you flip the steak, the part facing away from the direct heat can cool down and the center of the steak can absorb some of the built-up heat, allowing for a super even coast-to-coast pink.

Steakhouse: This method is basically the forward sear. When doing this, we sear a steak in a cast-iron or carbon steel pan, allow it to rest, then finish in a 250°F (120°C) indirect setup. It is a bulletproof method.

WHEN IS STEAK DONE?

We've cooked thousands of steaks at this point. And yes, we can typically push down firmly on the steak and tell you whether it is done by feel. But we use a thermometer. We can do math, but we use a calculator because it's a helpful tool. Thermometers are no different.

What is the perfect temp? That will differ from one person to the next. We like our steaks to land at 130 to 132°F (55 to 56°C) for medium-rare.

Regardless of where you want your steak, make sure you account for carryover heat. When a steak is on a 500°F (260°C) grill, the outside of the steak will absorb that energy. When you remove the steak from the grill, some of that energy will dissipate into the air and some will be absorbed by the cooler center of the steak, thus causing carryover cooking.

The amount of carryover will depend on the size of the steak and the temperature it is cooked at. The larger steaks, and steaks cooked at higher temperatures, will have the most carryover. Smaller steaks (less mass) and lower temps will result in lower carryover cooking.

For example, a 12-pound (5.4-kg) ribeye roast cooked at 450°F (230°C) could have fifteen degrees or more of carryover. A half-pound (227-g) sirloin cooked at 200°F (95°C) could have as little as two to five degrees of carryover.

The general rule of thumb: A steak that is cooked to your ideal final temperature on the grill will be overcooked on your plate. Plan accordingly!

HOW TO SLICE STEAK AND WHY IT MATTERS

Many amazing steaks are ruined by the knife.

When slicing a steak, the goal is to end up with the shortest muscle fibers possible. If you cut across, or perpendicular to, the grain, you will end up with just a small cross-section of the meat fibers, resulting in a super tender bite.

If you cut with, or parallel to, the grain, you end up with long muscle fibers that are completely intact, which will result in a super tough, shitty bite of steak.

REPETITION

If you want to master cooking steaks, you need to start simple, and cook over and over.

When you do this, you'll want to limit variables. Cook the same cut of meat, identical in weight, with just salt on the same part of the grill at the same temperature each time.

Once you get in the required reps, you will have a firm grasp of all the variables, like how long it takes to sear, the firmness of the meat at different levels of doneness, where to put the steak to avoid flare-ups, how long to rest it, etc.

Don't Cry for Me
ARGENTINIAN STEAK (PICANHA)
with Red Chimichurri

Serves: 6 | Prep Time: 60 minutes | Cook Time: 90 minutes

Since the inception of social media, we've seen food trends come in hot then slowly fade into the shadows, year after year. RIP, kale. . . . Picanha, however, came in hot but is here to stay. This cut, which was first celebrated in South America, is finally having its day here. And for good reason. It is as tender as a filet, as beefy as a sirloin and as marbled as a ribeye. It also features an iconic fat cap that is rich and smooth when cooked.

For the Steak

1 (2- to 2½-lb [907-g to 1.1-kg]) picanha steak

Kosher salt, for seasoning

Black pepper, for seasoning

Flaky salt, for finishing

For the Red Chimichurri

4 whole red bell peppers

2 chipotles in adobo

½ cup (30 g) roughly chopped fresh parsley

¼ cup (12 g) fresh oregano leaves

4 cloves garlic, smashed

¼ cup (60 ml) red wine vinegar

¼ cup (60 ml) olive oil

½ tsp kosher salt

1 tsp ancho chile powder

Pinch of crushed red pepper

Pat your picanha steak dry with paper towels. Flip the steak over so that the thick layer of fat is down against a cutting board. Use a sharp knife to trim away the steak's silverskin. Liberally season the steak all over with kosher salt and black pepper. Set the steak aside at room temperature for 1 hour.

Heat the grill for direct medium-high heat.

Wash and dry the red bell peppers. Set the bell peppers directly onto the grill. Turn the bell peppers every 2 to 3 minutes, until they are deeply charred and wrinkling. Remove the bell peppers to a bowl and cover with aluminum foil or a pot lid. Set aside for 5 minutes. After the bell peppers steam in their own heat, you can easily remove the charred skin, seeds and tops.

Lower your grill or smoker for indirect heat at low, about 225°F (110°C). Smoke the picanha steak for 75 to 90 minutes, or until the internal temp reaches 120°F (50°C). This is a good time to make the Red Chimichurri.

Combine the roasted bell peppers with the rest of the chimichurri ingredients in a blender and pulse until the parsley and garlic are chopped, and the sauce has thickened slightly. Don't overblend it! A coarse texture is ideal and shows off the peppers.

Remove the steak from the grill to a rimmed baking sheet to rest. Crank the heat up to 500°F (260°C). Return the steak to the grill and sear, turning every few minutes to prevent flare-ups from that juicy fat cap. When the steak is darkly seared and reaches an internal temp of 130°F (55°C) for medium-rare, remove it from the grill to rest for 10 minutes. Use a sharp knife to thinly slice the steak across the grain, season with a few pinches of the flaky salt and serve with the chimi.

Good Mojo Picón FLANK STEAK

Serves: 6, makes about 1 cup (240 ml) Mojo Picón | Prep Time: 20 minutes | Cook Time: 15 minutes

Flank steak is udderly delicious (Google "where on the cow is a flank steak" and you might get our joke). It's lean but has a big beefy flavor and stands up well to the grill. Two rules here. First, cook it hot and fast directly on the grill for maximum grilled flavor. Second, cut across the grain for maximum tenderness. Mojo Picón is a bright, fresh Spanish sauce with every element you need to jazz up your flank: heat, fat, punchy vinegar. Traditionally you would do this with a mortar and pestle, but we're speeding things up a bit.

For the Mojo Picón

8 cloves garlic

2 medium red chiles, picón or red serrano

1 tsp ancho chile powder

1 tsp ground cumin

1 tsp kosher salt

¾ cup (180 ml) olive oil

2 tsp (10 ml) sherry vinegar

For the Steak

2 lb (907 g) flank steak

Kosher salt, for seasoning

Black pepper, for seasoning

1 tsp ground cumin

¼ tsp ground coriander

Flaky salt, for finishing

To make the Mojo Picón, combine the garlic, chiles, ancho chile powder, cumin and salt in a food processor, and pulse until finely chopped, about twelve pulses. Scrape down the sides of the food processor, replace the lid and turn the food processor on. Drizzle in the oil until the sauce forms a smooth paste. Taste the sauce and adjust the seasoning, if necessary, before mixing in the sherry vinegar. Set aside while you grill the steak.

While we like to bring big, thick cuts of meat to room temp before grilling, keeping thin steaks like flank and skirt cold until just before grilling is extra insurance against overcooking over the flames.

Heat the grill to medium-high heat. While the grill heats, generously season the steak with kosher salt and black pepper on all sides. Combine the cumin and coriander in a small bowl, and sprinkle on the seasoned steak.

Grill the flank steak: You're going to grill this steak over medium-high direct heat, so keep it moving. Put the steak on the grill and cook for just 2 minutes on the first side before flipping, then keep flipping every 2 minutes until the steak is nicely charred, about 10 minutes total. We like an internal temperature of about 125°F (50°C) in the thickest part of the steak for rare. You can always use tongs to roll thinner sides of the flank up and away from the heat (like folding a tortilla) while you continue to cook the thicker end.

Remove the flank steak to a cutting board and rest for 10 minutes before slicing thinly across the grain. Season the sliced steak with the flaky salt and serve with a drizzle of the Mojo Picón.

LITTLE RED BAVETTE
with Real Herby Chimichurri

Serves: 6, makes about 1 cup (240 ml) chimichurri | Prep Time: 1 hour | Cook Time: 15 minutes

Some people, mostly on the internet, believe bavette and flank are the same steak. They're wrong. Bavette is actually from the bottom sirloin, a totally different "primal" section of the cow. We'll let the butchers and internet trolls work that out. For us, this steak cooks and tastes like the best parts of skirt steak and sirloin. You get the deep, deep beefy flavor of skirt with the girth of a sirloin. How you slice this cut will be the difference between a tender delight and delicious ball of rubber bands.

For the Steak

4 lb (1.8 kg) bavette, thick skirt or flap steak

Kosher salt, for seasoning

Flaky salt, for finishing

For the Real Herby Chimichurri

4 cloves garlic, chopped

¼ cup (35 g) green capers, drained

1 tbsp (15 ml) red wine vinegar

1 tbsp (15 ml) freshly squeezed lemon juice

½ cup (30 g) packed fresh parsley leaves

½ cup (12 g) packed fresh basil leaves

¼ cup (12 g) packed fresh oregano leaves

¼ cup (60 ml) olive oil

½ tsp kosher salt

½ tsp red pepper flakes

Remove the steak from the fridge at least an hour before cooking to take the chill off and get it to room temperature. Season well on all sides with kosher salt, and set aside while you prepare the chimi and grill.

Combine the garlic, capers, vinegar and lemon juice in the bowl of a food processor. Pulse three to four times to chop. Add the parsley, basil and oregano to the food processor, and turn on. Let the mixture form a thick paste before streaming in the olive oil. Stop the machine, scrape down the sides of the food processor bowl, and add the kosher salt and red pepper flakes. Pulse three to four more times to combine. Set aside.

Heat the grill to medium-high direct heat. When the grill is hot, cook the steak for 2 minutes over direct heat on the first side, then flip. Continue flipping and moving the steak every 2 minutes until it has a nice char and reaches an internal temp of at least 125°F (50°C) for rare, about 8 minutes total. Remove the steak from the grill and let it rest for 10 minutes before slicing. Season with the flaky salt and serve with the herby chimi.

"What've you got to lose?"

If you cook a steak in the forest . . .

can you see the tree fall?

Hanger-Over STEAK AND EGGS

Serves: 4, makes about 1 cup (240 ml) Pico de Gallo | Prep Time: 1 hour | Cook Time: 15 minutes

Hangover brunch is best met with steak, eggs and a bit of the hair of the dog that bit ya'. And maybe ibuprofen and electrolytes. We're not sure just how hard you hit it. The hanger steak often shows up as the star of our steak-and-eggs. It's like both sides of the porterhouse in one steak. Beefy, rich and tender. You can cook it quickly. And the best sauce for this? Yolk. When buying the hanger, you can get it whole or trimmed. A whole hanger requires some varsity knife skills to remove silverskin and sinew. We recommend having your butcher handle this. Especially if you don't remember who paid for the Uber.

For the Steak

1 (2-lb [907-g]) hanger steak

Kosher salt, for seasoning

Black pepper, for seasoning

For the Pico de Gallo and Eggs

1 small jalapeño, seeded and minced

1 large tomato, diced

1 tbsp (15 ml) lime juice

1 tsp kosher salt, divided

¼ cup (4 g) finely chopped fresh cilantro

2 tbsp (30 ml) olive oil

4 large eggs

Use a long, thin knife to remove any remaining silverskin and hard pieces of fat from the hanger steak. Season the steak on all sides with kosher salt and black pepper. Let the steak come up to room temperature for 1 hour while you make the Pico de Gallo, and prep the grill and eggs.

Combine the jalapeño, tomato, lime juice and ½ teaspoon of the kosher salt in a medium mixing bowl. Use a spoon to toss. Don't be gentle here; you want the tomato to release some juices. Add the cilantro and chill while you cook the steak.

Heat the grill to medium-high heat. Add the hanger steak and cook for 1 to 2 minutes per side. Here you aren't flipping the steak, but rather rolling it over with tongs to get a nice even sear all around, not just on four sides. In total, the hanger steak should be on the grill for 8 minutes to hit an internal temp of 125 to 130°F (50 to 55°C). With hanger steak, you really want to avoid overcooking. Let the steak rest for 5 minutes on a cutting board.

Meanwhile, heat the olive oil in a carbon steel skillet over medium heat until shimmering. Crack the eggs into a large bowl and carefully add to the pan. Season with the remaining ½ teaspoon of kosher salt and cook the eggs for 3 to 4 minutes, or until the whites are set and the edges are just beginning to brown. Remove from the pan. Slice the steak against the grain into thin pieces. Serve the steak with the eggs and Pico de Gallo—and possibly a little "hair of the dog" if you need it.

Steakhouse Upgraded: PORTERHOUSE

Serves: 2 | Prep Time: 1 hour | Cook Time: 90 minutes

Porterhouse: The ultimate blue-chip steak. A little bit country and a little bit rock and roll. The best of both worlds with two steaks in one. The iconic rich, beefy strip steak and the fancy-pants, melt-in-your-mouth filet mignon. And right at the heart of it is a big T-shaped bone adding flavor and setting you up for some terribly inappropriate bone jokes.

The difference between a T-bone and a porterhouse is the diameter of the filet side. The T-bone is much smaller. It's OK, T-bone; size isn't everything. Try pairing this with our Roasted Broccolini with Chiles (page 130).

For the Mâitre d'Butter

4 oz (113 g; 1 stick) high-quality butter, at room temperature

1 tsp lemon juice

1 tsp Dijon mustard

1 tbsp (4 g) finely chopped parsley

½ tsp kosher salt

For the Steak

1 (2-inch [5-cm]-thick) porterhouse steak, at least 2 lb (907 g) total

Kosher salt, for seasoning

Flaky salt, for finishing

You can make the Mâitre d'Butter several days in advance. Beat together the softened butter, lemon juice, mustard, parsley and salt in a medium mixing bowl with a spatula. Cut a piece of parchment paper to roughly the size of a sheet of printer paper. Spoon the butter across the length of the parchment—make sure you leave about 2 inches (5 cm) between the butter and the end of the paper. Roll the parchment over the butter and pull to round the butter into a log. Tightly wrap the remaining parchment around the log. You can also get creative with some inappropriate butter sculptures here. #butterdong

Remove the steak from the fridge at least an hour before cooking. Season the steak liberally with the salt as soon as it comes out of the fridge.

Heat the grill or smoker to low heat, about 250°F (120°C). Add the steak to the grill and cook until the internal temperature is 125°F (50°C), about 90 minutes. When it reaches temp, remove the steak from the grill and then increase the grill to high. Rest the steak for 30 minutes and when you're ready to serve, sear it for 2 minutes on each side.

For serving, you'll cut the porterhouse into two pieces—strip steak and filet mignon. Use a sharp knife to remove the steaks by cutting along the bone on each side. Slice each steak into ½-inch (1.3-cm) pieces and then return to their position around the bone. Season the steaks with a sprinkling of the flaky salt and top each side with a generous slice of the Mâitre d'Butter.

JUST THE TIP:

This steak can rest for up to an hour before searing, just tent it loosely with foil while it rests. If you are cooking for a crowd, start the steak a bit early, then sear right before you are ready to serve! No need to let it rest after searing!

TUSCAN TOMAHAWK
with Impressively Huge Bone

Serves: 4 | Prep Time: 24 hours | Cook Time: 2 hours

Yes, the bone is super thick and huge. Yes, your dinner guests will awkwardly gasp at the sight of it. Yes, we're serving this to compensate for anatomical shortcomings. But most importantly, this steak is fucking delicious. Season this bad boy heavy and early. Salting the day before gives the salt time to dissolve and get absorbed throughout the steak. With the big cuts, you want seasoning throughout, not just on the outside.

For the Steak

1 American Wagyu tomahawk ribeye, about 4½ lb (2 kg)

Kosher salt, for seasoning

Black pepper, for seasoning

2 tsp (3 g) garlic powder

For the Roasted Garlic Butter

2 heads garlic

2 tbsp (30 ml) olive oil

4 oz (113 g; 1 stick) salted butter, at room temperature

2 tbsp (6 g) finely chopped fresh oregano

Twenty-four hours before you plan to grill the steak, remove the steak from the fridge, set it on a cooling rack and set the cooling rack on a rimmed baking sheet. This setup will allow air to move around the steak while it dry brines. Season the steak liberally with kosher salt and black pepper on all sides, followed by the garlic powder. Refrigerate the steak, uncovered, for 24 hours before cooking.

Remove the tomahawk steak from the fridge at least an hour before cooking. While the steak comes to room temp, slice the tops off the garlic heads and set them inside a roughly 8 x 8–inch (20 x 20–cm) piece of foil. Drizzle the garlic heads with the olive oil and then close up the foil, making a tight package of garlic for slow roasting.

Heat the grill or smoker to low, about 250°F (120°C). Add the steak, along with the garlic packet, to the grill and cook until the steak reaches 125°F (50°C) and the garlic bundle can be easily squeezed with tongs, about 90 minutes. When the steak reaches temp, remove it from the grill, rest it for at least 10 minutes and then increase the grill to high. Sear the steak for 2 minutes on each side. Transfer the steak onto a cutting board and let it rest for 30 minutes. Remove the garlic from the grill and let it sit until it's cool enough to handle, about 10 minutes.

While the steak rests, squeeze that golden roasted garlic from its papery skin into a small mixing bowl, add the butter and oregano, and stir to combine.

Use a sharp knife to remove the meat from the tomahawk bone by cutting along the bone. Slice the steak into 1-inch (2.5-cm) pieces and then return the pieces to their position around the bone. Serve the tomahawk with the Roasted Garlic Butter.

PETITE TENDER: *The Steak Named After Us*

Serves: 6 | Prep Time: 1 hour | Cook Time: 30 minutes

The petite tender, aka the teres major, is a diamond in the rough sitting in the middle of the chuck roll. You get all the iconic chuck steak flavor and none of the gritty fat and connective tissue that is also synonymous with chuck. It's also the second most tender cut on the animal. Finally, a steak for the person that wants something super tender but is tired of getting made fun of by the waiter at the steakhouse for ordering a filet mignon.

For the Steak

2 petite tender steak (sometimes labelled teres major steak), about 2 lb (908 g)

Kosher salt, for seasoning

Flaky salt, for finishing

¼ cup (12 g) finely chopped fresh chives

¼ cup (15 g) finely chopped fresh parsley

For the Sour Cream Mashed Potatoes

3 lb (1.4 kg) Yukon gold potatoes, well-scrubbed

1 tbsp plus 2 tsp (30 g) salt, divided

4 oz (113 g; 1 stick) salted butter

1 cup (240 ml) sour cream

1 cup (240 ml) half and half

Remove the steak from the fridge and use a sharp knife to remove any visible silverskin. Season the steak on all sides with kosher salt. Set the tender at room temperature for at least an hour before grilling.

While the steak rests, go ahead and make the mashed potatoes. Set the potatoes in a large pot and cover with water by at least 1 inch (2.5 cm). Add 1 tablespoon (18 g) of the salt, cover the pot and set over medium-high heat. Bring the potatoes to a boil, uncover and cook for 20 to 25 minutes, or until fork tender. Drain the potatoes and let them cool slightly so you can remove their skins. Use a paring knife or a clean kitchen towel to slide off the skins. A potato ricer is really going to give you the smoothest, creamiest potatoes ever, so use that to mash the potatoes back into the pot or return the peeled potatoes to the pot and mash with a potato masher. Add the butter, sour cream, half and half and remaining 2 teaspoons (12 g) of salt, and combine over low heat on the stove. Remove the pot from the stove and cover while you cook the steak.

Heat the grill to medium-high heat. Add the steak and cook for 1 to 2 minutes per side. Here you aren't flipping the tender, but rather rolling it over with tongs to get a nice even sear all around, not just on four sides. In total, the tender should be on the grill for 15 minutes to hit an internal temp of 125 to 130°F (50 to 55°C). Let the steak rest for 10 minutes, loosely covered with foil on a cutting board.

To serve, spread a scoop of the Sour Cream Mashed Potatoes on a plate. Slice the steak into thin pieces across the grain. Top the potatoes with 3 to 4 slices of steak, and season with the flaky salt, chopped chives and parsley.

STEAKHOUSE STEAK SALAD
with a Not-From-London Broil

Serves: 8 | Prep Time: 24 hours | Cook Time: 30 minutes

We've been lied to. London broil is from Philly. And it's a technique, not a cut. When marinated and cooked perfectly, an inexpensive, unwanted cut transforms into the perfect juicy and tender centerpiece of a steakhouse salad. Also, this steak pairs better with blue cheese than a ribeye. Try to prove us wrong.

For the London Broil

¼ cup (60 ml) beer, we like something light like a lager

2 tbsp (30 ml) Worcestershire sauce

1 tsp red wine vinegar

1 tsp soy sauce

3 cloves garlic, minced

½ tsp red pepper flakes

¼ tsp cayenne pepper

1 (1½- to 2-lb [680- to 907-g]) London broil

For the Buttermilk Blue Cheese Dressing

⅓ cup (80 ml) buttermilk

⅓ cup (80 ml) sour cream

⅓ cup (80 ml) mayo

½ tsp salt

½ tsp pepper

¼ tsp Worcestershire sauce

8 oz (226 g) blue cheese crumbles, divided

For the Big Salad

2 large heads romaine, washed, rinsed and chopped

2 large avocados, peeled and sliced

1 small red onion, thinly sliced

4 oz (113 g) cherry tomatoes halves

4 large eggs, hard cooked

We like to marinate London broil overnight before grilling. In a large zip-top bag or baking dish, combine the beer, Worcestershire, red wine vinegar, soy sauce, garlic, red pepper flakes and cayenne. If you used a large bag, seal it and squish the mixture together. If you're marinating in a baking dish instead, whisk the marinade ingredients together. Add the broil to the marinade and marinate in the fridge for 24 hours, flipping the steak about halfway through the marinate time.

Before grilling the London broil, get all your salad fixings ready. Make the dressing by combining the buttermilk, sour cream, mayo, salt, pepper and Worcestershire in a small bowl. Whisk until smooth and then add half of the blue cheese crumbles.

Remove the broil from its marinade and pat it dry with paper towels. Let it come to room temperature for as long as possible (we'd say 2 hours, but our lawyer says 1 hour and 59 minutes for food safety reasons). While your steak comes to temperature, fill a large bowl with the romaine, avocados, red onion, tomatoes and peeled and halved eggs. Crumble the remaining blue cheese on top. Chill this while you cook the broil.

Heat the grill to medium-high direct heat (about 450°F [230°C]) and cook the broil, turning frequently until it reaches 128°F (53°C), about 15 minutes. Rest the steak, loosely covered, for 10 minutes. Sharpen your knife and slice the steak against the grain so thin it only has one side (or as thin as you can), and top the salad with the broil and blue cheese dressing.

SWANKY AF *Filet Roast*

Serves: 8 to 10 | Prep Time: 24 hours | Cook Time: 2 hours

It's time to spend 3 hours in the attic looking for your grandmother's special china that you didn't want because we're about to get fancy AF! This recipe is a bit involved and on the more expensive side, but it is a special occasion dish and totally worth the investment. And once you nail the technique of making your own beef tallow and using it as a flavor binder, you will never go back.

1 whole beef tenderloin, trimmed of surface fat and silverskin

Kosher salt, for seasoning

Black pepper, for seasoning

2 lb (907 g) beef fat trimmings

10–12 cloves garlic, about 1 whole head

6–8 stems rosemary, about 1 bunch

2 tbsp (7 g) dried rosemary

1 tsp garlic powder

2 stems rosemary, finely chopped

Flaky salt, for serving

JUST THE TIP:

Have your butcher tie back the skinny end of the roast and truss it for you. They won't do it? Get a new butcher. They suck.

For beef tenderloin, we prefer a king cut (thick slices) but a queen cut (thinly shaved slices) will give you that wedding buffet vibe.

Twenty-four hours before you plan to cook the roast, remove the roast from the fridge and set it on a cooling rack on a rimmed baking sheet. This setup will allow air to move around the roast while it dry brines. Season the roast on all sides with kosher salt and black pepper, and leave it uncovered in the fridge overnight.

While the roast is brining, prepare the garlic-rosemary fat for coating the roast. Add the beef fat to a tall narrow pot and set it over low heat. We usually do this inside since you'll cook the beef fat for about 4 to 4½ hours at this temperature, stirring every 30 minutes or so. Your beef fat is finished when the beef pieces are mostly covered by the clear fat and are slightly browned. Set a large fine-mesh strainer over a large bowl and carefully pour the fat through the strainer. Add the garlic and rosemary stems, and cool to room temp. Keep at room temp overnight.

The next day, prepare your smoker with an indirect smoke at 225°F (110°C). We like cherry, hickory or oak, in that order of preference, for smoking tenderloin.

Combine the dried rosemary, garlic powder and 1 teaspoon of black pepper in a small bowl. This is the rosemary seasoning you'll use just before smoking.

Heat up the beef fat over medium-low heat on the stove. While the tenderloin is still cold from the fridge, use a pastry brush to coat the roast with a thick layer of the warmed-up garlic-rosemary beef fat. After you brush some on, quickly sprinkle on some of the rosemary seasoning. The tallow will quickly set, locking the rosemary onto the surface of the roast. Repeat until the entire roast is covered.

Cook the roast for 1 to 1½ hours, until it reaches 130°F (55°C). Let it rest for 30 minutes, or up to 1 hour before you're ready to serve. Brush the roast with additional garlic-rosemary fat again before searing. Crank the smoker to high heat and sear over direct high heat for 4 to 5 minutes per side. Rest briefly for 5 minutes and then drizzle with warm fat, finely chopped rosemary and the flaky salt just before serving.

Fancy Pants RIBEYE ROAST BEAST

Serves: 8 to 10 | Prep Time: 24 hours | Cook Time: 6 hours

This is a mic drop–worthy holiday centerpiece. The giant, perfectly marbled, coast to coast pink rib roast. When choosing your roast beast, choose a bone-in cut, and ask your butcher to cut off the bone plate and tie it back on. This allows you to get seasoning behind the bones, which will greatly improve the flavor throughout. We recommend blasting "Kashmir" on 11 and walking into the dining room in slow motion for serving.

For the Steak

1 (10-lb [4.5-kg]) prime ribeye roast

Kosher salt, for seasoning

½ cup (120 ml) Dijon mustard

¼ cup (60 g) prepared horseradish

6 cloves garlic, minced

¼ cup (7 g) finely chopped rosemary

For the Horseradish Sauce

⅓ cup (80 ml) buttermilk

⅓ cup (80 ml) sour cream

⅓ cup (80 ml) mayo

⅓ cup (80 ml) prepared horseradish

1 tbsp (15 ml) lemon juice

½ tsp kosher salt

½ tsp black pepper

¼ tsp Worcestershire sauce

Twenty-four hours before you plan to smoke the roast, season it all over with kosher salt. If your butcher removed the bones for you, season the entire roast and the ribs with the salt before tying the ribs back against the roast with butcher's twine. If your butcher tied the ribs to your roast, do your best to get the salt down in between these two hunks of meat. Set the roast on a rack set inside a rimmed baking sheet and refrigerate for at least 24 hours.

Remove the roast from the fridge about 1 hour and 59 minutes before you plan to cook it. In a small bowl, combine the mustard, horseradish, garlic and rosemary. Slather this mixture on the rib roast.

Heat the smoker to low heat—225°F (110°C). Set the roast in the smoker and cook to 120°F (50°C) for rare; this will take about 5 to 5½ hours for a 10-pound (4.5-kg) roast. When it hits the temperature, remove the roast from the smoker and crank the heat to high.

While the grill heats up, make your Horseradish Sauce by whisking the buttermilk, sour cream, mayo, horseradish, lemon juice, kosher salt, black pepper and Worcestershire sauce in a small bowl.

When the grill has heated to high, return the roast to the grill to get a nice sear and help it hit temperature. Aim for 130°F (55°C) for rare, 135°F (57°C) for medium-rare and 140°F (60°C) for medium. Rest the roast off the grill for at least 15 minutes before slicing and serving with the Horseradish Sauce.

JUST THE TIP:

The rough math for timing a roast is 35 minutes per pound (454 g), so if your roast is smaller, check it sooner. Also, if you are cooking this to medium-well or higher (we forgive you) cook it at the lower temp until it hits 130°F (55°C) instead of 120°F (50°C). Also, don't do this.

Eva's Ancho Chile-Rubbed
SKIRT STEAK TACOS

Serves: 3 to 4 | Prep Time: 2 hours and 15 minutes | Cook Time: 20 minutes

These are my favorite tacos to make! When I make them for guests they sometimes look at the dish's name and exclaim, "I don't like spicy!" but I always assure them that the chili powder adds only a beautiful color and nice flavor. I promise it does not *pica*, as my Aunt Elsa would say, meaning that it's not spicy.

For the Tacos

2 lb (907 g) skirt steak, cut into strips

3 tbsp (45 ml) olive oil

3 tbsp (45 ml) lime juice

4–5 cloves garlic, thinly sliced

1–2 serrano peppers, sliced

1 tsp cumin

2 tbsp (11 g) ancho chili powder

½ tsp kosher salt

12 corn tortillas

For the Guacamole

3 ripe avocados, diced

2 medium ripe tomatoes, seeded and diced

1 small white onion, finely chopped

¼ bunch fresh cilantro, chopped

½ serrano pepper, finely minced

2 small lemons, juiced, about 4 tbsp (60 ml)

1 tsp kosher salt

Place the skirt steak in a medium-sized bowl. Pour the olive oil and lime juice over the skirt steak. Add the garlic, serrano peppers, cumin, ancho chili powder and kosher salt. This will be your marinade. Massage the marinade into the meat with clean hands, then cover with plastic wrap. Place in refrigerator for a minimum of 2 hours.

While the steak marinates, mix your guacamole. In a large bowl, combine the avocados, tomatoes, onion, cilantro, serrano peppers, lemon juice and kosher salt. Taste and add more kosher salt, if desired. Transfer to a serving bowl.

Lightly oil your grill grate with a neutral oil and heat the grill to medium-high. Add the steak directly to the grates and cook, turning once, 3 to 5 minutes per side for medium-rare. Transfer the steak to a cutting board and let it rest for 5 minutes.

Cut the steak diagonally across the grain into thin strips. Stack the tortillas on a cutting board and use a sharp, thin-bladed knife to trim them into 4-inch (10-cm) squares. Heat the tortillas on a comal, or a flat cast-iron griddle over medium heat, until warm and soft. Transfer to a plate for serving.

Place 2 to 3 strips of steak across the center of the tortilla. Garnish with guacamole. Pull the diamond-shaped tortilla together corner to corner (so it looks like a triangle), and secure it with a toothpick. Repeat for additional tacos, and serve.

WE'RE BRINGING
POULTRY
Back. Yeah.

Poultry gets a bad rap. But we are here to show you that
it's more than just an obligatory back-up dish at a barbecue for your two dipshit friends that don't eat red meat. It
is more than just a bland, dry, healthy alternative. When
you buy the correct bird, season it properly and apply
simple and sound cooking techniques,
a bird can be the main event.

Bachelors of Science
in Chicken

WHICH BIRD IS THE WORD?

Selecting poultry is super simple. There aren't that many options. Here is what we look for. And don't be shy about branching out and trying some of the local heritage birds at your farmers' market. They actually have flavor.

Free range: This is essential for us. There is a saying, whose origin we don't remember, that goes, "Never eat an animal that didn't live a life worth living." For this, free range is a must.

Air chilled: When poultry is slaughtered, it needs to rapidly cool down. The typical way producers handle this is by putting the chicken in a supercooled water-based solution. This unfortunately results in waterlogged skin. And because we all know that moisture is the enemy of crispy, this is not ideal. Air chilled never sees this water bucket and is much easier to work with.

Not brined: If you see the words "contains up to XX% of a solution," then that chicken has been brined. It has been loaded up with a solution of water and salt to increase its sale weight and hide the fact that it is bland AF. We like to get the natural, unbrined birds and control the seasoning ourselves.

DRY BRINE IT

We could do an entire book just on dry brines. In fact, we have an entire line of dry brines with Spiceology for sale on our website. Why? Because they're everything.

Here is the short version . . .

What does dry brining do? The salt in the brine wicks out moisture from the poultry, which dissolves the salt. Then, the salt solution is reabsorbed into the meat. This is where the salt does its magic by denaturing, or breaking down, the proteins. This makes sure the proteins don't constrict during cooking (which squeezes out their own juices), and it leaves you with extra tender and juicy meat that is seasoned throughout.

There is a common misconception that wet brining makes for a moist bird because the liquid is absorbed, making it seem juicier. This is false. The liquid is just the vessel for getting salt in the bird to denature the proteins, exactly how it works with dry brining, but without an annoyingly clunky, fussy, messy process that includes dealing with 6 gallons (23 L) of poultry water that leaked in your garage.

The final benefit is super crispy skin. We dry brine in a fridge, uncovered. This allows any excess moisture in the skin to evaporate. This tight and dry skin gets super crispy during cooking. The wet brine fails here as well because you are left trying to crisp up incredibly waterlogged skin.

WHEN IS THIS BIRD DONE?

We are only working with chicken and turkey for this book. And according to the FDA, they are both members of the 165°F (75°C) doneness club.

By now, you've already figured out that we aren't scientists or doctors. So legally, we tell you to listen to those people. Consuming raw or undercooked poultry could have potential negative side effects. And if you have any concerns, cook it to 165°F (75°C).

Okay, enough of that.

The key here is to learn about carryover temp. Understand it. Then use it to your advantage. Carryover temp is easy to grasp. Shit keeps cooking for a bit when it comes out of the oven or off the grill.

For us, that means if you leave poultry on the grill until it hits 165°F (75°C), it will be 175°F (80°C) when it gets to the plate. The result? Dry, overcooked poultry. You might as well throw it in the trash and order a pizza. Only bone-in chicken thighs can survive this mistreatment.

The bigger the bird, and higher the cooking temp, the more carryover cooking. If we are roasting a giant turkey at 350°F (175°C), we will pull it off between 145 and 150°F (63 and 65°C). For a whole chicken we will pull it off between 150 and 155°F (65 and 68°C) in the breast. If you have a Meater thermometer, it will calculate carryover cooking for you and give you an exact temperature at which to remove the bird. Small pieces, like skin-on, bone-in thighs can go right to 160°F (70°C).

The Very Best GRILLED CHICKEN EVER

Serves: 4 to 6 | Prep Time: 40 minutes | Cook Time: 35 minutes

We heard that in fancy culinary schools, the first thing they teach you is how to make amazing chicken with just salt. We weren't admitted to any of those schools so we can't confirm. Regardless, this chicken recipe is intentionally simple and intentionally first in the chapter to establish some fundamentals. Oh, and also to make epically delicious chicken.

The word count is high on this recipe, but it is mainly about how to buy a whole chicken and break it down. We personally find this process therapeutic. Don't let it scare you off. You can get a butcher to do this or buy the parts already separated.

For the Chicken

1 (4- to 5-lb [1.8- to 2.3-kg]) broiler fryer chicken or 4 lb (1.8 kg) skin-on, bone-in pieces

Kosher salt, for seasoning

Black pepper, for seasoning

2 tsp (10 g) granulated sugar

1 tsp garlic powder

If you master breaking down a whole chicken into pieces, then you can save money and give everyone the BBQ chicken piece they love. Here's how to do it, and make sure to check out our photo series on the next pages (52–54).

With a sharp chef's knife and a large cutting board ready, pat the chicken dry with paper towels.

Starting with one side, grab the drumstick and pull it away from the chicken, until the skin is taught. Use the knife to cut through the skin between the leg and the body, then repeat on the other side. Pull the leg down farther and twist it hard until the leg joint pops out of the socket. Flip the bird over and score the top of the skin above and between the thighs. Then use your knife to remove the leg quarter by cutting through the joint area you revealed. Repeat this on the other side. Working with one quarter at a time, you can split the thigh and drumstick by placing the piece skin side down and locating the joint. There's often a white piece of fat between the thigh and drumstick that you can use as a guide or you can use your fingers to feel around for the joint. Separate the pieces by cutting directly through the joint and repeat with the other quarter.

For the Texas BBQ Sauce

1½ cups (360 ml) ketchup

½ cup (120 ml) apple cider vinegar

½ cup (120 ml) water

¼ cup (55 g) light brown sugar

¼ cup (60 ml) honey

1 tbsp (5 g) cayenne pepper

2 tbsp (28 g) butter

Removing the wing is just as easy as removing the leg. Pull the wing taut away from the breast. Cut through the joint to remove the wing and repeat on the other side. Cut through the joint, as you did with the thighs, to remove the wing tip. Save these for making stock.

Lastly, remove the chicken's breasts. Flip the body back over and use the knife to cut through the skin on the sternum. Keeping your knife as close as possible to the rib bones, slice off the breasts on each side. You can turn the carcass into stock, so don't throw it away!

Set the chicken pieces on a rack set inside a rimmed baking sheet. Season each piece well with kosher salt and black pepper. Then combine the sugar and garlic powder in a small bowl, and stir to combine. Season the chicken pieces on all sides with this seasoning mixture and dry brine, uncovered, in the fridge for 24 hours before grilling.

Make the sauce by combining the ketchup, apple cider vinegar, water, sugar, honey and cayenne in a medium pot. Bring to a boil over medium-high heat, then reduce the heat to medium, add the butter and cook for about 10 minutes. The sauce will be thin. Store for up to 3 days in advance of cooking.

Heat the grill for two-zone cooking, with the heated side cranked to high. Cook the chicken over indirect heat for 18 to 20 minutes. Keep close to the grill to move the chicken as needed to prevent flare ups and rotate the pieces away from the high-heat side of the grill. When the chicken reaches 150°F (65°C), you can begin basting with the sauce. Sauce the chicken every 2 to 3 minutes for an additional 10 to 12 minutes until the breasts hit 160°F (70°C). Serve with any remaining sauce and lots of napkins.

(continued)

JUST THE TIP:
This is our basic BBQ recipe, but you can switch things up by swapping the cayenne for chipotle, habanero or your favorite heat. Or get citrusy and use orange juice in place of the vinegar.

Make sure the chicken is dry

Turn it sideways

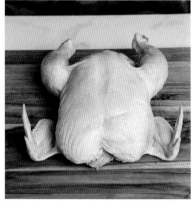

Why do we keep turning the chicken?

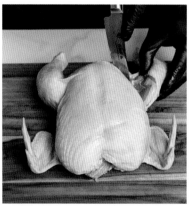

Cut the skin between the leg and breast

Cut through the joint

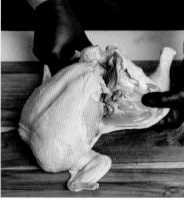

Bend the legs back to separate the joint

Flip it over and flop the legs around to make it dance

Score the top of the skin above the thighs

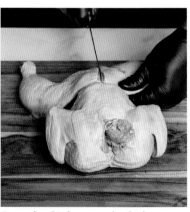

Score the skin between the thighs

Pick up the leg and cut through on the bottom

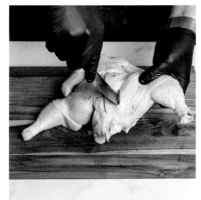

Flip over and finish cutting through the skin

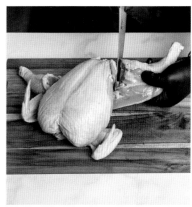

Repeat

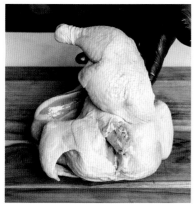

Display the leg to a camera person

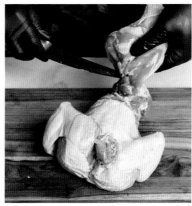

Remove the other leg

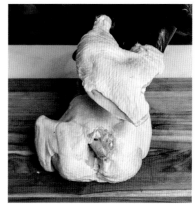

Also display this to a camera person

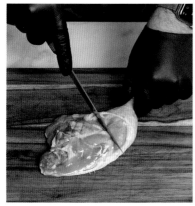

Flip the leg quarter over and find the line above the joint

Cut through to separate the leg and thigh

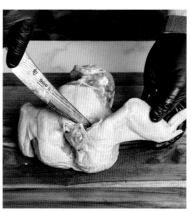

Pull back the wings to expose the joint

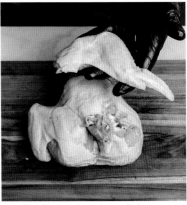

Trim the skin, and cut through the joint to remove the wings

Remove the tip

Score the skin between the two breasts

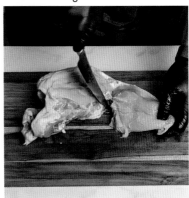

Slice the breast off, staying as close to the bone as possible

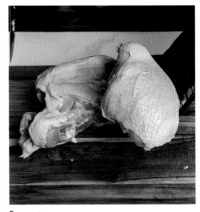

Repeat

Place them on a fancy rack

Better Than BUFFALO CHICKEN WINGS

Serves: 4 to 6 | Prep Time: 24 hours | Cook Time: 90 minutes

This is no dig on the actual wings from Buffalo (which are just called wings there). We're talking about the wings at thousands of bullshit sports bars around the country that are soggy, sad and fried in the same oil as the fish and chips. Gross. We dry brine these wings then smoke them to render out excess fat and provide some smoke flavor, grill them for an epic char, then pan fry them for skin that is so crispy it breaks like glass. And the sauce? The perfect combo of sweet and heat.

For the Wings

3 lb (1.4 kg) chicken wings, split into flats and drumettes

Kosher salt, for seasoning

Black pepper, for seasoning

1 tbsp (8 g) cornstarch

2 tsp (9 g) baking soda

2 tbsp (30 ml) avocado oil

For the Ranch Crema

½ cup (120 ml) crema

¼ cup (60 ml) buttermilk

¼ cup (12 g) finely chopped chives

¼ cup (15 g) finely chopped fresh parsley

1 clove garlic, minced

1 tsp kosher salt

½ tsp black pepper

For the Hot Honey Sauce

½ cup (120 ml) light honey

⅓ cup (80 ml) hot sauce (Tapatío, Texas Pete's or Crystal)

4 cloves garlic, minced

4 tbsp (56 g) salted butter, at room temperature

A day before you plan to eat them, generously season the wings on both sides with kosher salt and black pepper. Spread the wings out on a drying rack set inside a rimmed baking sheet. Combine the cornstarch and baking soda in a small bowl, and then use a fine-mesh strainer to dust the mixture onto both sides of the wings. Chill the wings, uncovered, for 24 hours.

You can make the Ranch Crema just before serving, or a day in advance. Combine the crema, buttermilk, chives, parsley, garlic, kosher salt and black pepper in a medium bowl. Whisk to combine, cover and chill for at least 30 minutes before serving.

Set a smoker or grill for smoking at low, about 250°F (120°C). We like cherry or a blend for this. Smoke the wings directly on the grates until they reach 150°F (65°C), roughly 60 minutes. Remove the wings from the grill and set the grill to medium-high heat, about 450°F (230°C). Return the wings to the grill over direct heat. Your goal is a good char, about 2 minutes per side. Move the wings off the grill and mix up the sauce by combining the honey, hot sauce, garlic and butter in a small bowl. Have this standing by.

Next step is to get those wings nice and crispy. Heat a wok over medium-high heat (this can be done on the grill, the stovetop or the side burner, if you've got it). When the wok is hot, add the avocado oil, followed directly with the wings. The trick here is to keep the wok and wings moving. As soon as the skin on the wings begins to bubble, add the sauce mixture and keep tossing until the sauce has thickened. Immediately remove the wings from the wok onto a cooling rack—this will keep them crisp while they cool enough to pick up. Serve the wings hot with the cool crema for dipping.

CHICKEN *Saltimbocca*

Serves: 4 to 6 | Prep Time: 12 hours | Cook Time: 35 minutes

Chicken can stand up to big flavors. Sage and prosciutto are no exception. Classic saltimbocca is a dish typically made with cutlets in a pan. We thought it was time for a grill upgrade by using bone-in, skin-on thighs and turning the insanely delicious pan sauce into a compound butter. This allows you to get the smoke and char flavor from the grill without losing any of the delicious flavor from the sauce.

2 lb (907 g) bone-in, skin-on chicken thighs, about 8 total

¼ lb (113 g) thinly sliced prosciutto

Kosher salt, for seasoning

2 tbsp (30 ml) olive oil

8 sage leaves

4 cloves garlic, minced

¼ cup (60 ml) white wine

2 tbsp (30 ml) lemon juice

½ tsp red pepper flakes

4 oz (113 g; 1 stick) salted butter, divided

Remove the chicken from the fridge and pat dry with paper towels. Using your fingers and a paring knife, gently pull up the chicken skin in the middle of each thigh—you want to create a pocket by keeping the skin attached at the sides. When the pieces are all prepped, carefully place a piece of prosciutto under the skin of each thigh. Liberally sprinkle the thighs all over with kosher salt. Dry brine these pieces on a cooling rack set in a rimmed baking pan overnight in the fridge.

Before you get to grilling the chicken, make a super flavorful compound butter with all the flavors of saltimbocca. Heat the olive oil over medium heat on the stovetop—you can use a cast-iron or non-stick pan for this. Add the sage leaves and fry until crispy, about 3 minutes total. Remove the sage leaves to a paper towel to drain. Add the garlic, wine, lemon juice and red pepper flakes, and reduce the heat slightly. The mixture should bubble, reduce by half and soften the garlic. Pour this mixture off into a heatproof bowl and cool for 10 minutes. Add half of the butter to the warm mixture—it will melt but get super flavorful. Then cool for an additional 20 minutes before mixing in the remaining butter. You can tightly roll this into a log (see page 33) and chill for serving.

When you're ready to cook the chicken, heat the grill for two-zone cooking, with the heated side cranked to high. Cook the chicken over indirect heat until the thighs reach 165°F (75°C), about 25 to 30 minutes. Stay close to the grill to move the chicken as needed to prevent flare-ups and rotate the pieces away from the high heat side of the grill. Move the chicken to the high heat side of the grill and cook until charred, about 3 minutes. Remove the chicken from the grill and top each piece with a slice of the compound butter and a fried sage leaf.

CHICKEN PAILLARD SO THIN
It Only Has One Side

Serves: 4 to 6 | Prep Time: 20 minutes | Cook Time: 25 minutes

Paillard, which roughly translates into, "pounded thin by the hooves of virgin unicorns," is a summertime weeknight favorite for us. It is juicy, bright, refreshing and cooks fast.

4 chicken breasts

Kosher salt, for seasoning

Black pepper, for seasoning

¼ cup plus 1 tbsp (75 ml) olive oil, divided

1 small red onion, diced

2 cups (300 g) cherry tomatoes

2 large lemons, halved

5 oz (142 g) baby arugula

¼ cup (15 g) finely chopped fresh parsley

Flaky salt, for finishing

Remove the chicken breast from the fridge and pat dry with paper towels. Use a sharp knife to butterfly each breast—place your hand on the breast and slice through it starting at the thickest part to cut it in half horizontally. Working with one filleted breast at a time, cover the breast with plastic wrap and use a mallet to pound the thickest sections to about ¼ inch (6 mm) thickness. Season the paillard pieces on all sides with kosher salt and black pepper, and set aside.

Heat the grill to medium-high heat. Set a pan over the heat and add 1 tablespoon (15 ml) of the olive oil, the onion, tomatoes and a few pinches of kosher salt. Cook until the tomatoes burst and the mixture is jammy, about 10 minutes. Remove the pan from the heat.

Grill the chicken and lemons (cut side down) over direct heat. After 2 minutes, rotate the chicken 45 degrees. After 2 more minutes, flip and repeat. Remove the chicken and the lemon halves from the grill; it should reach 165°F (75°C).

Quickly toss the salad. In a large serving bowl, toss together the remaining ¼ cup (60 ml) of olive oil, juice from 1 whole grilled lemon, arugula and parsley. Season with a pinch of kosher salt and toss again. Top each chicken breast with the tomato mixture and a sprinkle of flaky salt with a generous serving of salad. Slice the remaining grilled lemon halves into wedges and serve with the chicken.

Not Your Grandma's Dry
TURKEY AND STUFFING

Serves: 10 to 12 | Prep Time: 24 to 48 hours | Cook Time: 2 hours

Just because your mom served you an overcooked, dry, bland megamart bird with squishy stuffing that was neither delicious nor food safe doesn't mean you should give up on turkey. This spatchcock technique solves lots of problems, including uneven cooking. Notice there is no gravy recipe attached. That's because it's juicy AF and won't need salty cornstarch goop to make it tolerable.

Turkey is back. You're welcome.

For the Turkey

1 (12- to 14-lb [5.4- to 6.4-kg]) whole, natural turkey

Kosher salt, for seasoning

Black pepper, for seasoning

¼ cup (50 g) maple sugar

2 tbsp (28 g) brown sugar

1 tbsp (7 g) ancho chile pepper

1 tbsp (7 g) sweet paprika

You can totally ask your butcher to spatchcock your turkey for you, but it is also easy to do at home. Make sure your turkey is completely thawed, and the neck and giblets are removed. Start by patting the turkey dry with paper towels. Set the turkey backbone up on a cutting board with the drumsticks closest to you. Use a heavy pair of shears to cut out the backbone; set your non-dominant hand on the turkey to steady it and work up one side of the backbone at a time. After you've removed the backbone (save it for turkey stock) flip the turkey over and press both hands against the breast plate to flatten the turkey—a couple of audible cracks means you've done it.

Be generous with the kosher salt and season with black pepper liberally on every bit of the turkey, including the backside of the bird and under the skin. Then combine the maple sugar, brown sugar, chile pepper and sweet paprika in a small bowl (see the shameless plug on the next page). Season the turkey with this mixture and then set the bird on a cooling rack, set inside a rimmed baking sheet. Dry brine the turkey for at least 24 hours but ideally 48 hours, uncovered in the fridge, skin side up.

(continued)

For the Sausage and Fennel Stuffing

1 lb (454 g) hot Italian sausage, bulk or removed from its casing

1 large sweet yellow onion, thinly sliced

1 large head fennel, stemmed and coarsely chopped

2½ cups (600 ml) chicken broth

4 large eggs

1 tbsp (3 g) finely chopped fresh sage

1 tbsp (3 g) finely chopped fresh thyme

2 tsp (10 g) kosher salt

1½ lb (680 g) bakery croutons

Make the stuffing in advance too; you can bake it on the grill while the turkey rests the next day. Heat the grill to medium heat (or a similar temp on an indoor burner) and place a large cast-iron skillet over the grate. Brown the sausage in the hot skillet until mostly cooked through and some of the fat has been released. Add the onion and fennel, and cook until very soft, about 12 minutes. While the onion and fennel cooks, whisk together the chicken broth, eggs, sage, thyme and salt—a large, spouted measuring cup is best for this. Add the croutons to the sausage—fennel mixture, and pour the brothy mixture over the whole pan. Use a sturdy wooden spoon to make sure that everything is coated well and then press the mixture into the pan. Cover the pan with foil and stash in the fridge until you cook the turkey.

Remove the turkey from the fridge for 1 hour and 59 minutes before you begin. Take the stuffing out of the fridge then, too.

Set the grill or smoker to high heat (aim for 450 to 500°F [230 to 260°C]). Set the turkey directly on the grates, skin side up, and cook until the skin is beginning to turn golden and crisp, just 12 to 15 minutes. Reduce the grill's heat to medium (aim for 300°F [150°C]) and cook until the turkey reaches 145 to 150°F (63 to 65°C) in the breast, about 90 minutes. Remove the turkey to a clean cooling rack and rest, loosely covered with foil, for about 25 minutes.

While the turkey rests, cook the stuffing. Uncover the pan and set the stuffing on the grill. Cover the grill and cook until the stuffing is browned and reaches 140°F (60°C) internal temp, about 25 minutes.

Carve the turkey. Remove the breasts and slice the breast into ½-inch (1.3-cm)-thick pieces. Cut between the drumsticks and thighs to remove, and then slice the thigh meat into ½-inch (1.3-cm) pieces as well. Serve with the stuffing.

A SHAMELESS PLUG FROM MARK AND FEY:

This is already a spice blend we make with Spiceology that is designed just for poultry. If we were you, we'd just order it at Spiceology.com.

Pineapple Juice Can TURKEY

Serves: 10 to 12 | Prep Time: 24 hours | Cook Time: 4 hours

Pacific flavors pair perfectly with plump poultry. So why should turkey be any different? We've upgraded the beer can to a pineapple can to provide the structural integrity needed for the bigger bird. This method gives you all the benefits of the beer-can method, resulting in evenly cooked, juicy turkey. Put it all together and you have a salty, sweet, spicy, fruity, crispy and juicy turkey.

For the Turkey

1 (10- to 12-lb [4.5- to 5.4-kg]) natural turkey

Kosher salt, for seasoning

½ cup (110 g) light brown sugar

2 tbsp (17 g) garlic powder

2 tbsp (11 g) ground ginger

1 (20-oz [567-g]) can pineapple rings in 100% juice

Make sure your turkey is completely thawed and that the neck and giblets are removed. Pat the inside and outside dry with paper towels and season abundantly with kosher salt inside and out. Mix the sugar, garlic powder and ground ginger, and season the turkey with this mixture. Set the turkey on a cooling rack inside a baking sheet and chill, uncovered, for 24 to 48 hours.

Before you cook the turkey, prep the can and sauce. Begin by opening the can of pineapple rings, and removing the rings from the pineapple juice. You can grill the pineapple rings along with the turkey or save them for our Pineapple Bacon Jam (page 138). Pour off 1 cup (240 ml) of the juices for the sauce, and set aside. Remove the paper label from the can and add 1 cup (240 ml) of water to any remaining juices and pineapple bits in the can. Set this aside while you prepare the sauce.

(continued)

For the Polynesian Sauce

1 cup (240 ml) pineapple juice, reserved from can of pineapple rings

½ cup (120 ml) soy sauce

¼ cup (60 ml) lime juice

¼ cup (60 ml) lemon juice

2 tbsp (30 ml) honey

3 tbsp (18 g) grated fresh ginger

4 cloves garlic, grated

2 scallions, finely sliced

2 tsp (3 g) crushed red pepper

Pour the reserved pineapple juice into a medium saucepan and bring to a boil over medium heat. Reduce the pineapple juice by half, then add the soy sauce, lime and lemon juice, honey, ginger, garlic, scallions and crushed red pepper. Bring back to a boil, and cook until thickened and reduced, about 15 minutes.

Heat the grill for medium, indirect heat. Aim for an internal grill temp of 325 to 350°F (165 to 175°C).

Set the pineapple can inside a metal 8 x 8–inch (20 x 20–cm) baking pan. NSFW: Slowly lower the turkey, leg side down, onto the can until it is securely propped upright. Place the pan over indirect heat (over the turned-off burners or where there are no coals). Cover and grill until the turkey reaches 150°F (65°C), about 2½ hours.

Baste the turkey with the Polynesian Sauce and continue to cook, covered, basting every 10 minutes, until the skin is deeply colored, crisp and a probe thermometer in the deepest part of the thigh registers 160°F (70°C), 45 to 60 minutes more.

Remove the turkey and the pan with its drippings from the grill. (If you are using a foil pan, slide the pan onto a baking sheet before moving it around.) Let the turkey rest for at least 20 minutes.

To remove the turkey from the pineapple can, first move the turkey—still on the can—to a clean cutting board. Have one person keep a firm grip on the can to hold it in place (careful, it's hot!) while a second person grasps the turkey with wadded paper towels or a clean kitchen towel and pulls it off the can. Carve and serve with any additional sauce.

Smoky CHICKEN NOODLE SOUP

Serves: 4 to 6 | Prep Time: 20 minutes | Cook Time: 30 minutes

Chicken soup is great as it is. But that doesn't mean we can't make it fucking fantastic. The addition of a smoky layer of flavor on the chicken and the finishing touch of lemony, bright, herbaceous, garlicky gremolata sure does kick it all up a notch. There is only one problem with this dish. Now when you tell your grandmother that her chicken noodle soup is your favorite, you'll be lying. What kind of person are you? Wow.

You'll notice we're skipping a dry brine here, and that's (1) because we are using only chicken thighs, the juiciest of chicken parts and (2) because everything is going in a broth where it will get more seasoning and moisture.

For the Smoky Chicken Soup

1½ lb (680 g) bone-in chicken thighs, about 6

Kosher salt, for seasoning

3 large carrots, peeled and chopped

3 stalks celery, chopped on the bias

1 large yellow onion, chopped

6 cups (1½ qt; 1.4 L) chicken broth, divided

9 oz (255 g) fresh pappardelle or fettuccine, cut into ½-inch (1.3-cm) pieces

For Grandma's Gremolata

1 cup (60 g) fresh parsley leaves

2 cloves garlic

1 large lemon, washed and dried

½ tsp kosher salt

3 tbsp (45 ml) olive oil

Heat the grill or smoker to medium-high, about 350°F (175°C). Season the chicken thighs well with kosher salt and set on a rimmed baking sheet. Add the carrots, celery and onion and season them with a three-finger pinch of kosher salt. Smoke the chicken and vegetables on the tray until the thighs are cooked through and the vegetables are almost tender, about 25 minutes.

Remove the chicken from the baking sheet and set aside. Move the vegetables to a large Dutch oven. Use ½ cup (120 ml) of the chicken broth to deglaze the baking sheet: Pour the broth onto the still hot pan and use a wooden spoon to scrape off any cooked-on bits. Pour this into the Dutch oven and add the remaining broth. Chop the chicken thighs into bite-sized pieces and add them to the Dutch oven. Cover the Dutch oven, and close the grill and bring to a boil over medium-high heat. While the soup heats, make the gremolata.

Use a chef's knife to finely chop the parsley. Grate the garlic cloves onto your pile of parsley, and then use the same grater to zest the lemon onto the parsley as well. Season with the kosher salt. Chop through the pile of parsley two to three more times to combine. Move the gremolata to a bowl and stir in the olive oil.

Add the fresh pasta noodles to the Dutch oven and cook for just 2 minutes before serving. Spoon the soup into bowls and serve with a spoonful of gremolata.

Itty Bitty Chickie Committee
CHICKEN ROULADES

Serves: 4 to 6 | Prep Time: 45 minutes | Cook Time: 60 minutes

Chicken breast gets a bad rap for being bland and boring—mainly because it normally is. The roulade allows you to introduce ribbons of salty, nutty, creamy flavor throughout. And the reverse sear results in a juicy and tender chicken with a crispy, crunchy skin. You can prep these a day in advance and cook for a crowd.

2 tbsp (28 g) salted butter

1 large red onion, thinly sliced

Kosher salt, for seasoning

5 oz (142 g) fresh baby spinach

4 boneless, skin-on chicken breasts

3 oz (85 g) thinly sliced prosciutto

7 oz (198 g) Fontina cheese, grated

Vegetable oil, for seasoning

1 batch Red Chimichurri (page 23)

Heat the smoker or grill to low, about 250°F (120°C).

Melt the butter in a large pan over medium heat on a stovetop or a side burner of your grill. Add the red onion, season with a pinch of kosher salt and cook, stirring regularly, until caramelized, about 20 minutes. Remove the onion from the pan and add the spinach. Cook until wilted and most of the moisture is cooked out, 3 minutes. Remove the spinach to paper towels to drain. Set aside while you prepare the chicken.

Remove the chicken breasts' skin by carefully pulling between the skin and the flesh; you can use a paring knife or shears to detach the skin as needed. Set the skin aside to use later. Working with one breast at a time, place a chicken breast on a cutting board. Cover with plastic wrap and pound with a meat mallet to about a ¼-inch (6-mm)-thick square. Remove the plastic wrap and repeat with the remaining breasts. Pat the chicken breasts dry with paper towels and season each generously with kosher salt.

Again, working with one breast at a time, layer on the filling ingredients in this order: two pieces of prosciutto, ⅓ cup (50 g) of the Fontina cheese, ¼ each of the spinach and caramelized onion. Starting from a short end, roll the chicken into a log. Tuck in any loose bits. Wrap the whole roulade with the reserved skin and tuck it in along the edges. Secure the roll with kitchen twine.

Rub the roulades all over with a pinch of kosher salt and drizzle of vegetable oil, and transfer to the smoker/grill at 250°F (120°C) until an instant-read thermometer inserted into the thickest part of the roulades reads 150°F (65°C), about 35 minutes.

Move the chicken roulades to a platter or cutting board. Increase the heat to 475°F (245°C). Return the roulades to the smoker, and cook for 10 to 12 minutes more to crisp the skin and get to an internal temperature of 160°F (70°C). Rest the roulades for 15 minutes before removing the twine and thinly slicing each into ½-inch (1.3-cm) pieces. Serve with the Red Chimichurri.

Ye Ole TURKEY LEGS

Serves: 8 to 10 | Prep Time: 24 hours | Cook Time: 3 hours

We aren't going to admit in writing that we like medieval castles and poorly staged jousting matches. But we will commit to giant turkey legs and swords. These are simple, insanely delicious and travel well. Oh, if you have some churrasco swords, this is the time to use them. Because . . . swords.

8–10 turkey legs, about 12 oz (340 g) each

Kosher salt, for seasoning

½ cup (110 g) brown sugar

3 tbsp (25 g) garlic powder

3 tbsp (21 g) onion powder

3 tbsp (8 g) dried thyme

3 tbsp (6 g) dried sage

1½ tbsp (9 g) black pepper

1 tbsp (7 g) smoked paprika

1 tsp ground nutmeg

1 tsp ground allspice

At least a day before smoking, season your turkey legs handsomely with kosher salt on all sides. Combine the sugar, garlic powder, onion powder, dried thyme, dried sage, black pepper, smoked paprika, nutmeg and allspice in a small bowl. Season the turkey legs all over with the spice mixture and stash the legs in a large roasting pan to dry brine overnight in the fridge.

Remove the turkey legs from the fridge at least 1 hour before you plan to smoke them. If you're going to roast these, thread them on the sword while still cold from the fridge. (Oh, you don't have a spare roasting sword lying around? My bad, didn't realize you were a loser . . .)

Our preference for smoking these legs is hot coal smoking in a charcoal grill. Heat one charcoal chimney worth of lump charcoal to white ashy hot—this will take about 40 minutes. Set a small aluminum drip pan in the center of your grill and pour the lit charcoal around the pan. Fill the drip pan with water and add two handfuls of hickory chips directly to the coals. Add the grill rack over the coals and place the turkey legs around the center. You may need to add more chips or coals to maintain an even heat around 250°F (120°C). Smoke the legs for 2½ to 3 hours.

Alternatively, use a smoker if you got one. Set it up for low heat with hickory; you want to maintain a temperature between 240 and 260°F (115 to 125°C). Smoke the legs for 2½ to 3 hours. Rest the legs for at least 10 minutes before serving.

JUST THE TIP:

So, this recipe calls for a lot of legs, but these babies freeze beautifully, which means you can have smoked turkey later for making robust pots of beans, collard greens and soups anytime you'd like.

THIS LITTLE
PIGGY
Went on the Grill

Let's talk about pork, baby. Although the pork people tried to trick us into thinking it was white meat, pork is actually red meat and, if done right, is one of the most versatile and best-tasting proteins on the planet. And on Mars or in other pig-friendly galaxies as well.

Cooking with pork is all about choosing the right cut, understanding the right temperature to cook that cut to and knowing how to season it. From low-and-slow pork shoulder to pounded pork loin, you can get really creative when using this spectacular ingredient.

So, let's take a little journey down piggy lane and see if we can't inspire you to take another look at pork and make some mind-blowing dishes worthy of the main attraction at any affair.

Pig Facts

HOW TO BUY PORK

When you are buying pork at your local grocery store or butcher shop, there are a few important things to keep in mind. First, if the package doesn't show where the pork is from, you might want to ask someone to clarify. Locally sourced pork is ideal, but make sure it is at least from a reputable brand or company.

Pork producers and the USDA have worked hard to make pork cleaner and safer. The pork you're buying now isn't the scary pork we had as kids.

Pork can vary from extremely lean to heavily marbled. Since fat equals flavor, consider your cuts carefully. Higher quality pork will have fat that is more evenly dispersed and is soft enough to melt in your fingers at room temperature.

Also, look for meat that has a reddish or pinkish color but without any liquid in the package. Liquid could mean that the pork is a bit past its prime and therefore should be avoided. Also, the meat should be firm to the touch without any "mushy" areas.

A LITTLE PINK IS SAFE TO EAT (AND TASTY TOO)

You might have grown up, like us, eating dry, dusty pork chops because our parents grew up afraid of undercooking pork. Trichinosis—a parasite that used to cause a lot of illness—was the main reason so many folks were afraid of pink pork. The good news is that trichinosis cases have all but disappeared in the last 40 years thanks to better pig farming and food handling. Even the USDA has changed its recommendations on the best temperature for serving pork cuts like tenderloin and chops.

From the USDA: "Cook all raw pork steaks, chops and roasts to a minimum internal temperature of 145°F (62.8°C) as measured with a food thermometer before removing meat from the heat source. If fresh pork has reached 145°F (62.8°C) throughout, even though it may still be pink in the center, it should be safe. The pink color can be due to the cooking method or added ingredients."

So, in other words: If you cook pork to 145°F (63°C), you are good to go. But, when we get a great piece of pork that is organic and locally sourced, we tend to cook many cuts of pork to 135 to 138°F (57 to 59°C) to ensure that it's tender and delicious with great moisture and flavor.

OUR GO-TO PORK PARTS

Now let's talk about cuts of pork. Here are a few of the most common cuts and our "go to" when it comes to creating recipes that create a musical of porky proportions on your plate and on your palette. And that's a lot of P's.

Pork Chop

One of the oldest, most incredible and go-to cuts that we use in our cooking arsenal on a regular basis, the pork chop is a loin cut and taken from the rib area of the pig. Basically, it's perpendicular to the spine and therefore a much leaner cut than others. Many times the pork chop is served bone-in, but you can also find boneless versions that are both thick or thin, depending on the cut. These can be cooked as is or how we enjoy doing it—pounding them out thin for pan frying, grilling or even breading and deep-frying. Eat these with a beautiful sauce and a side of veggies for a perfect individual meal or make a bunch for a crowd. Either way, they are a winner in our book.

Pork Tenderloin

The pork tenderloin is one of our absolute favorite cuts of any meat, not just pork. This cut is also referred to as a pork fillet, a pork tender or—as we like to call it—The Gentleman's Cut. The tenderloin is the long, thin muscle that runs along the central spine of the animal.

We think the pork tenderloin is the Willy Wonka Factory of the pig. This is the cut of pork where your creativity can be king—you can literally stuff it with anything, and you can experiment with a variety of flavors and textures. If there was ever a cut of meat to play around with, this would be the one.

Try stuffing a pork tenderloin with cooked bacon, cream cheese, jalapeño and caramelized onions (then tying it up with butcher's twine), conveniently described for you in our Jalapeño Popper Stuffed Pork Tenderloin recipe on page 80. Once you try this, you might cook tenderloin 8 days a week.

Pork Loin

This cut of meat is probably one of the most common types you will find in a grocery store. Pork loin is typically sold whole or sliced thin and can come in both boneless and bone-in forms.

Unlike the pork tenderloin, which runs along the animal's backbone, the pork loin actually comes from the upper back portion of the animal. Pork loin is extremely versatile and perfect if you want to make a quick meal for your family or something that doesn't require a lot of prep work or marinating, and can be cooked in a variety of ways.

This easy-to-cook protein can be roasted or sliced and pounded thin, deep fried, breaded, sautéed, pan fried or grilled. Serve with a savory sauce or a side of potatoes or freshly grilled veggies, like our Roasted Broccolini with Chiles (page 130).

Pork Shoulder and Collar

You might know the pork shoulder as a pork butt or Boston butt. The pork collar, referred to as the money muscle, is the neck-side portion of this cut and can be cooked the same ways you'd cook a shoulder. These cuts are in the same general area but are all butchered a bit differently. However, and for the most part, these are easy substitutes and are cooked basically the same way.

Because of the volume of the meat, the extensive fat content and connective tissue contained in each cut, this cut of pork requires a low-and-slow method either on a smoker, braised or roasted in an oven or even stewed and simmered on a stovetop in a Dutch oven or stock pot. This is also perfect for a slow cooker, which will give you plenty of time to drink beer while waiting for it to be finished.

Additionally, to retain moisture for maximum enjoyment, these cuts need to cook to 203 to 207°F (95 to 97°C) to render the fat and break down the connective tissues. Typically, when people have dry and tough pulled pork, it is actually undercooked.

You'll know this type of cut is done when it is probe tender. At this point it can easily be sliced or most commonly, pulled. Yep, you got it—pulled pork. This cut is also used as a grind to make sausage and other types of ground pork products (the notable fat content helps prevent drying out and adds incredible flavor when ground up).

This cut comes from the front part of the animal with a pork butt being located higher up on the foreleg versus the shoulder, which is a bit farther down. However, the flavor profile is almost identical and therefore can be used interchangeably in recipes. So go HOG WILD and experiment.

Pork Ribs

As one of the most common cuts of pork and the one that takes the piggy cake at the tailgate, pork ribs are one of the tastiest and best cuts of meat you can get. This "eat-it-with-your-hands" delicious cut comes from, yeah, you guessed it, the rib cage of the animal.

Pork ribs are typically packaged in large sections and are almost always bone-in—which means meat and bones come together—and that's just how you cook them.

There are several different styles of ribs, but the two main ones are baby back and spare ribs. Spare ribs are fattier and have a more pronounced flavor. Baby back ribs are lean and tender.

Ribs are one of most popular cuts of pork and can be cooked by grilling, smoking or baking, and in many cases, all three! One thing to watch out for is the membrane. When you buy pork ribs at a local store or butcher, kindly ask them to remove the membrane that runs down the backside of the rib portions. The membrane is a tough and rubbery film layer that helps to hold the bones to the meat on the backside of the cut. Although many people forget or just leave it on, we always prefer to take it off. It's easy enough to just take a towel and "peel" it away from the bones in one long piece.

This cut of meat is also most commonly served with some type of sweet, spicy or savory BBQ sauce or dry rub. You really can't go wrong with this baby.

THREE LITTLE PIGGIE (TYPES) WENT TO MARKET

You might have heard about some different types of premium pork from Berkshire, Kurobuta or Iberico pigs. These are the best of the best when it comes to quality and, quite honestly, have some of the best flavor that you can put in your mouth. Here are a few things to look for when using one of these three types of pigs.

Berkshire

Berkshire pigs are a breed that originated in England and are considered extremely rare and a delicacy because of their incredible juiciness, tenderness and flavor. Berkshire pigs tend to be more marbled than other types and have a beautiful pinkish color to them that makes them perfect for a low-and-slow type of cooking. But, you can also use this cut for rapid cooking, pan searing or frying.

Kurobuta

One of our absolute favorite types of pork, Kurobuta is the name for a Japanese heritage breed of pigs that literally means "black pig." The Japanese used pure-bred English Berkshire pigs that were black in color but introduced a different feeding method that resulted in a more uniform marbling and moisture retention. Basically, Kurobuta pork can be considered the Wagyu of pork.

The most influential and best-known producer of this breed of pig is from Kagoshima, which crosses a British Berkshire pig with a domestic black pig. Again, this rare breed has an incredible texture and flavor profile, making it one of the most standout proteins you can get. We encourage you to take a ride on the Kurobuta train and take that baby all the way to "holy shit this is good" town.

Iberico

¡Que rico! This literally means "delicious" in Spanish, and you know what? That's exactly what this type of pig is: delicious!

This pig's heritage is something out of the history books. In fact, it can be traced back to the time of the cavemen who inhabited the Iberian Peninsula. This is what makes this animal so special, and it can't be found anywhere else in the world.

These pigs have the life. Found only in Spain, they are free range and eat an amazing diet of local grains as well as acorns. It's their rich diet of acorns that in turn gives them an incredible marbling and fat content that is rich and considered "nutty" in flavor. This is where jamon Iberico comes from and is a staple in all parts of Spain and exported globally.

If you can get your hands on Iberico pork, do it. Trust us. You won't regret your decision.

Jalapeño Popper Stuffed PORK TENDERLOIN

Serves: 4 to 6 | Prep Time: 24 hours | Cook Time: 35 minutes

This recipe (and cut of meat) is all about being stuffed! And we are going to stuff it with things that traditionally go inside a jalapeño popper. We are going to use a butterflied tenderloin as the vessel to hold cheese, onions, peppers, spices and honey, and wrap the whole damn thing with bacon. Why? Because bacon.

Make this for a large crowd or do what Mark does: Make one just for yourself and have a good cry because of how tasty it is.

For the Pork

2 pork tenderloins, about 2 lb (907 g) total

Kosher salt, for seasoning

Black pepper, for seasoning

1 tsp red pepper

1 tsp ancho chile powder

1 tsp smoked paprika

1 tsp garlic powder

Start this epic tenderloin by butterflying and dry brining the pork. Working with one tenderloin at a time, carefully remove any silverskin from the outside of the tenderloin and then slice it in half lengthwise (like a hot dog bun). Repeat with the second tenderloin. Cover the tenderloins with plastic wrap and then use a meat mallet to pound the butterflied tenderloins into a thin, even layer. Season the tenderloins on both sides with kosher salt and black pepper. Combine the red pepper, ancho chile powder, smoked paprika and garlic powder in a small bowl, and season the tenderloins on both sides with the spice mixture. Move the tenderloins to a sheet pan and cover them with plastic wrap. Dry brine these pieces for at least 4 hours in the fridge but preferably overnight.

(continued)

Jalapeño Popper Stuffed **PORK TENDERLOIN** *(continued)*

For the Filling and Bacon Wrap

2 tbsp (30 ml) olive oil

1 medium yellow onion, sliced into rings

Kosher salt, for seasoning

4 medium jalapeños, cored and sliced into rings

8 oz (226 g) cream cheese, cubed and chilled

1 cup (113 g) shredded sharp Cheddar cheese

1 tbsp (15 ml) honey

Black pepper, for seasoning

1 (9.5-oz [269-g]) bag Fritos®, divided

12 slices thick-cut bacon, about 12 oz (340 g)

Pickled jalapeños, for serving

Ranch Crema (page 56), for serving (optional)

You can make the filling about 1 hour before you plan to cook the tenderloin, or the night before. Heat a large skillet over medium-high heat on the stove and add the olive oil, followed by the onion and a pinch of kosher salt. Cook until the onion starts to soften, about 4 minutes. Add the jalapeños, and cook until the onion and jalapeños are both charred. Remove the onion and jalapeños to a cutting board, and cool while you prep the rest of the filling.

In a medium bowl, combine the cream cheese, Cheddar and honey. Season with a three-finger pinch of kosher salt and black pepper. Roughly chop the charred onion and jalapeños, then add these to the bowl of cream cheese, and mix to combine. The mixture may be a little soft from the warm vegetables, so pop it in the fridge for 5 minutes before you fill the pork. Crush 1 cup (40 g) of the Fritos (this will go inside the tenderloins) and save the rest for garnishing.

Set yourself up for filling and rolling the pork. On a piece of plastic wrap, line up 6 slices of bacon and place one of the seasoned, flattened tenderloins on top—the longest part of the tenderloin should be closest to you with the bacon pieces running perpendicular. Sprinkle the tenderloin with ½ cup (20 g) crushed Fritos. Dollop half of the cream cheese mixture across the length of the tenderloin, leaving a 1-inch (2.5-cm) space closest to you. Roll the pork up over the cream cheese—don't worry about rolling up the bacon yet. Do your best to get a tight, even roll. Once the pork is wrapped onto itself, roll the whole thing back toward you, this time wrapping the bacon as you go. Tightly wrap the tenderloin in the plastic wrap and chill while you repeat with the other tenderloin, and then heat the grill.

Prepare a grill for two-zone cooking on medium-high. The key here is to crisp the bacon without overcooking the pork. So, start with a cold tenderloin. Add the tenderloins to the hot side of the grill and cook until the bacon is beginning to crisp, about 10 minutes. Move the tenderloins to indirect heat and cook until they reach an internal temp of 140°F (60°C), about 15 to 20 minutes more.

Rest the tenderloins for 10 minutes before slicing into 1-inch (2.5-cm) pieces. Garnish with the crumbled Fritos, pickled jalapeño peppers and a drizzle of Ranch Crema, if desired.

Vinnie Bagaziti's **BONE-IN TOMAHAWK PORK CHOP PARM**

Serves: 4, makes 2 cups (480 ml) Red Sauce | Prep Time: 90 minutes | Cook Time: 50 minutes

Look, if you are gonna go big, you might as well get some tomahawk bone-in pork chops to impress your guests. This is one of those "oh no you didn't" recipes that will make you the talk of the next Zoom meeting. The key to this delicious and hearty dish is to season it every step of the way, starting with the meat and throughout the dredging process.

You might as well make four or more, because the work is about the same as making just two. So, get after it and don't skimp. We top the whole thing with a fresh and robust Sheet-Pan Red Sauce to bring in some earthy notes to your savory, nutty and subtly sweet Parmesan pork chop. This recipe will get you laid.

GUYS: This is potentially a false claim and we really can't be promising this to people!

For the Sheet-Pan Red Sauce

3 lb (1.4 kg) Roma tomatoes, halved and seedy pulp scooped out

Kosher salt, for seasoning

¼ cup (60 ml) olive oil

10 cloves garlic, smashed

1 small white onion, thinly sliced

1 tsp red pepper flakes

1–2 tsp (5–10 g) sugar

1 small bunch fresh basil

Prep the Sheet-Pan Red Sauce first; you can even do this up to 3 days in advance. Heat the grill for medium-high heat (about 400°F [205°C]). Cover a rimmed baking pan with foil (see Tip). Arrange the Roma tomatoes with the cut side up and season generously with about two three-finger pinches of kosher salt. Drizzle the tomatoes with the olive oil and stick a garlic clove inside as many tomatoes as you can. Toss the onion onto the pan as well. Roast this sheet pan of veggies on the grill to soften and concentrate their flavor, about 30 minutes.

Remove the pan from the grill and cool for about 20 minutes, then move the vegetables to a blender. Add the red pepper flakes, a pinch of kosher salt and the sugar. Blend until smooth then taste, adding additional salt or sugar as needed. Then toss in the basil and pulse to chop.

(continued)

Vinnie Bagaziti's **BONE-IN TOMAHAWK**
PORK CHOP PARM *(continued)*

For the Pork Chop Parmesan

4 bone-in tomahawk pork chops, about 12 oz (340 g) each

Kosher salt, for seasoning

Black pepper, for seasoning

1 tsp garlic powder

1 cup (125 g) all-purpose flour

2 large eggs

1 cup (108 g) Italian breadcrumbs

½ cup (28 g) panko breadcrumbs

2 oz (57 g) finely grated Parmesan cheese, plus more for serving

1 cup (240 ml) olive oil, divided

2 tbsp (28 g) salted butter, divided

8 oz (226 g) fresh mozzarella

¼ cup (15 g) finely chopped fresh parsley

To prepare the chops, working with one at a time, pound the pork chops with the tenderizing side of a meat mallet to double the size of each one. Season the pork chops generously with kosher salt, black pepper and garlic powder. Set aside while you set up for breading the chops.

Set up a breading station using three shallow dishes. Fill the first with the all-purpose flour, seasoned with a pinch of kosher salt. Fill the second with the eggs, lightly beaten with a fork and seasoned with a pinch of kosher salt. The third dish is for the final step of the dredge. Fill it with the Italian breadcrumbs, panko breadcrumbs and Parmesan cheese. Coat each of the pork chops by pressing into the flour, dipping in the egg (make sure both sides get good coverage), and then really press the chops into the breadcrumb mixture to coat. Set the chops aside on a cooling rack—air circulation will help the breading set while you get ready for frying.

Set yourself up for success by having the warm red sauce, mozzarella and additional Parmesan ready before you begin frying. You'll also want another rimmed baking sheet covered with foil and a clean cooling rack on top for finishing the pork chop Parmesan.

Heat a large cast-iron skillet over medium-high heat on the grill. Add ½ cup (120 ml) of the olive oil and 1 tablespoon (14 g) of the butter to heat. Fry one to two pork chops at a time, depending on the size of your pan—they'll cook quickly, about 4 minutes per side. Move the finished pork chops to the cooling rack on a sheet pan. If you need to, wipe out the skillet, and add the remaining olive oil and butter between batches. Repeat with the remaining pork chops.

When all four chops are fried, top each pork chop with a big-ass spoonful of red sauce and lots of fresh mozzarella, and return the pan to the hot grill to melt the cheese. Finish with the additional Parmesan (we recommend a ton, like a *Scarface* amount) and fresh parsley.

JUST THE TIP:
Covering your sheet pan with foil will significantly cut down on the amount of scrubbing you'd have to do; ask us how we know.

Char Siu PORK RIBS

Serves: 6 to 8 | Prep Time: 2 hours | Cook Time: 3 hours

These pork ribs will have you screaming "Ohhh Mommy!" Or umami. Whichever one.
This is one Chinese dish that brings all the flavors to the forefront and combines them
with a sticky, sweet, savory and salty sauce. Adding some fresh scallions to bring in
that earthy and bitter flavor alongside the crunch and sweetness of peanuts will
create a freaking EDM rave in your mouth.

For the Ribs

4 lb (1.8 kg) baby back pork ribs, about 2 racks

Kosher salt, for seasoning

1 tsp garlic powder

1 tsp ginger powder

1 tsp allspice

½ tsp ground fennel

½ tsp cayenne pepper

For the Sauce

½ cup (120 ml) orange juice

½ cup (120 ml) hoisin, we like Lee Kum Kee

¼ cup (60 ml) Shaoxing wine or sherry vinegar

1 tbsp (15 ml) soy sauce

1 tsp sesame oil

For the Crispy Shallots

6 large shallots

1½ cups (180 ml) vegetable or peanut oil

½ cup (60 g) finely chopped peanuts

1 bunch scallions, light green parts only, finely chopped

Remove the membrane from the back of ribs—otherwise your ribs will be tough and chewy no matter how long you cook them. Flip the racks over so that the bones are facing up. Pry a finger (or a spoon) between the silvery membrane and the ribs to start pulling up the membrane—we like to do this between two of the rib bones. Once you have a piece of membrane pulled up, you should be able to easily pull the whole membrane off; use paper towels to grip this slippery membrane as needed.

Season the ribs liberally with kosher salt. Combine the garlic powder, ginger powder, allspice, fennel and cayenne in a small bowl, and sprinkle this mixture all over the ribs. Wrap in foil and chill for 2 hours.

Heat the grill on high for two-zone grilling—we're looking for about 400°F (205°C). Cook the ribs, wrapped in the foil, over indirect heat until the meat is pulling away from the bone, 45 minutes to 1 hour.

Make the sauce and shallots while the ribs cook. Bring the orange juice to a boil over medium-high heat in a small saucepan and reduce by half. Whisk in the hoisin, Shaoxing wine, soy sauce and sesame oil, and remove from the heat.

Peel and thinly slice the shallots on a mandoline. Move the shallots to a colander or fine-mesh strainer and rinse well to soften. Add the shallots to a medium-sized saucepan and cover with the oil—you may not need to use all the oil. Set the pan over medium heat on the stovetop, and bring the shallots and oil to a simmer. Stir the shallots often and cook until browned, about 25 minutes. Drain the shallots into a fine-mesh strainer set over a heatproof bowl (you can save this delicious oil for another use). Turn the crispy shallots out onto paper towels to drain and season with a pinch of kosher salt.

When the ribs are tender and pulling away from the bone, remove them from the grill. Use tongs (the ribs will be hot) and a sharp knife to cut the ribs into two-bone sections. Coat the ribs with the sauce and return the ribs to the grill, this time over high heat to caramelize the sauce, about 4 minutes total in time. Remove the ribs from the grill and cool for about 5 minutes before topping with the fried shallots, peanuts and scallions.

Pull up the membrane

Grab it with a paper towel

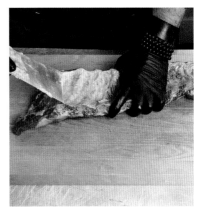

Rip it off

BBQ PULLED PORK COLLAR *Baked Potato*

Serves: 8 | Prep Time: 24 hours | Cook Time: 6 hours

Now this is a recipe that calls for popp'n collars. Know what we mean? Hahaha. Right? Sorry . . . Anyway, we love this recipe because it puts a subtle twist on a pulled pork dish that typically would use a pork shoulder or pork butt. Pork collar, which is from the same general area of the pig, has a more defined marbling and the flavor profile is in maximum overdrive. It's a perfect cut of meat cooked low and slow letting the fat render and the moisture stay inside the protein—something that will pay dividends when you stuff your baked potato with it. Plus, grilling the potatoes to finish them will give you an incredible smoky profile and complement the richness of the pork perfectly.

For the Pork

1 whole pork collar, about 4 lb (1.8 kg)

Kosher salt, for seasoning

Black pepper, for seasoning

Garlic powder, for seasoning

1 cup (240 ml) Texas BBQ Sauce (page 51), or your favorite local bottle, plus more for serving

For the Twice-Grilled Potatoes

4 large russet potatoes, scrubbed and rinsed

1 cup (240 ml) sour cream, plus more for serving

1 cup (113 g) sharp Cheddar cheese, divided

½ cup (50 g) finely grated Parmesan

4 tbsp (56 g) salted butter

3 large scallions, finely chopped, plus more for serving

Kosher salt, for seasoning

Black pepper, for seasoning

Crispy onions, for serving, store-bought or use the crispy shallots from page 86

Pat the pork collar dry and season all over with kosher salt, black pepper and garlic powder—we can't tell you how much, measure that shit with your heart. Dry brine this overnight, uncovered in the fridge or tightly wrapped in plastic; just remember to turn your wrapped collar about halfway through brining.

Remove the pork collar from the fridge. Set a smoker to low heat (we like hickory for this). Add the collar directly to the smoker, and cook low and slow until it is probe tender, the internal temperature will be close to 207°F (98°C); this will take 4 to 5 hours. Remove the collar from the grill, cool it for 10 minutes and wrap tightly in butcher paper to rest for an hour while you prep the potatoes.

Jump-start the potatoes by microwaving them. Pierce the potatoes all over with a fork and set them in a microwave-safe dish. Microwave at full power for 5 minutes. Use tongs to flip and cook for an additional 5 minutes. Continue to microwave at one-minute intervals as needed, until the potatoes are fork tender. Set aside to cool while you prep the filling mixture.

In a large mixing bowl, combine the sour cream, ½ of the Cheddar cheese, Parmesan, butter and scallions. Season with a heavy pinch of kosher salt and black pepper. When the potatoes are cool enough to handle, cut them in ½ lengthwise, scoop out the tender potato insides (leave about ⅛-inch [3-mm] of potato in the skins for structure) and add this to the bowl. Use a potato masher to mix and smooth this filling. Scoop ½ cup (150 g) of the mixture back into each of the potatoes and arrange on a rimmed baking sheet. Top each potato with some of the remaining Cheddar cheese.

Increase the heat of the grill or smoker to high. Cook the potatoes until they are warmed through, and the cheese is melted and browned, about 15 minutes. While the potatoes cool, shred the pork and toss it with the BBQ sauce.

Pile the pork on top of the finished potatoes, drizzle with additional BBQ sauce, crispy onions, scallions and finish with a dollop of sour cream.

Kālua PIG BOWL

Serves: 6 to 8 | Prep Time: 12 to 24 hours | Cook Time: 5 to 6 hours

Aloha! Thanks for flying Hawaiian Foodways. This traditional, yet inspired Hawaiian dish is the comfort food you didn't even know you needed in your life. Well, welcome to the Kalua Pig Bowl—come on in, the water's great. This recipe combines salty and savory pork with the sweet and earthy flavor found in teriyaki sauce. Add in some fragrant jasmine rice and bean sprouts for texture, and you've got a meal fit for the whole family. Oh, and if you want to make this super fast and simple, get some SPAM. It works great and happens to be one of the Hawaiian islands' most delicious ingredients. And it's in a can. Which is cool.

For the Pork

5 lb (2.3 kg) pork shoulder aka pork butt

Kosher salt, for seasoning

Black pepper, for seasoning

½ cup (120 ml) orange juice

½ cup (120 ml) water

1 (3-inch [7.5-cm]) piece fresh ginger, sliced

For the Teriyaki Sauce

½ cup (120 ml) orange juice

¼ cup (60 ml) soy sauce

3 tbsp (42 g) brown sugar

3 tbsp (45 ml) honey

3 cloves garlic, grated

2 tbsp (12 g) freshly grated ginger

For Serving

Cooked jasmine rice, about 6 cups (960 g)

6–8 eggs, fried (optional)

3 tbsp (24 g) toasted sesame seeds

1 bunch scallions, chopped

2 medium jalapeños, seeded and thinly sliced

2 cups (210 g) fresh bean sprouts

The day before smoking, generously season the pork shoulder with kosher salt and black pepper. Dry brine in the fridge for 12 to 24 hours. We like to do this right on the roasting rack in the roasting pan that we'll use on the grill.

Make the Teriyaki Sauce up to 3 days in advance. Bring the orange juice to a simmer in a small saucepan on the stovetop set over medium-high heat and reduce by half. Add the soy sauce, sugar, honey, garlic and ginger, and cook until thickened and reduced slightly, about 10 minutes.

Prepare a smoker for low-and-slow cooking with applewood for smoking the shoulder. Before you add the shoulder to the smoker, pour the orange juice, water and ginger into the bottom of the roasting pan. Smoke the shoulder between 275 and 300°F (135 and 150°C) until super tender, roughly 5 hours. You'll know it is done when the probe thermometer feels like it is going into room-temp butter or reads somewhere between 202 and 207°F (94 and 97°C). Remove the shoulder from the smoker and tightly wrap in heavy-duty foil or butcher's paper to rest for an hour before shredding; this is a good time to cook the rice and fry the eggs (if using) for serving. Reserve the roasting pan juices for topping the bowl.

Serve the shredded pork over rice with the pan juices and Teriyaki Sauce. Sprinkle each bowl with sesame seeds, scallions, jalapeños and sprouts, and serve with a fried egg on top, if desired.

Pounded ta Hell PORK CHOP SAMMY

Serves: 6 | Prep Time: 25 minutes | Cook Time: 20 minutes

Have you ever thought to yourself: "Self, I would like to have a super thin, pounded pork sandwich that has some mustard and crunchy arugula on crusty bread"? Yeah, us too. This super simple sandwich was inspired by our trips to Spain where it is called *bocadillo de lomo* (pork sandwich). It has just the right amount of meat-to-bread ratio, and is the perfect quick and easy lunchtime snack. Or, make a bunch for a hungry crowd. Enjoy.

6 boneless pork chops

Kosher salt, for seasoning

Black pepper, for seasoning

½ cup (120 ml) olive oil

¼ cup (60 ml) red wine vinegar

½ tsp Dijon mustard

½ tsp kosher salt

1 clove garlic, grated

1 large shallot, thinly sliced

5 oz (142 g) arugula

6 Kaiser rolls or other crusty bread

Pat the pork chops dry with paper towels. Working with one chop at a time, cover the chop with plastic wrap and pound with a meat mallet like it owes you money. Repeat with the remaining pork chops and then season the chops well with kosher salt and black pepper.

Heat the grill for high direct heat. Add the chops and cook for 2 to 3 minutes on each side—you want to brown the pork chops without overcooking them. Rest the cooked chops on a plate for 5 minutes while you throw together a salad.

Whisk together the olive oil, red wine vinegar, mustard and salt in a large serving bowl. Add the garlic and shallot, and toss to coat. Finally add the arugula and massage to coat the greens. If you've got some juices from the rested chops, pour those into this bowl too. Build your sandwiches by adding a pork chop and generous heap of salad to each split Kaiser roll.

PRO TIP:
Pair with ice cold beer.

INTERNATIONAL
MEN OF MYSTERY

(Can We Have Spy Theme Music Here?)

We've traveled all over the world. What do we remember
the most? The food. Followed by the great beer. Followed
by the tiny hotel rooms and the constant confusion about
how tipping works. We digress . . .

We're big-time fans of international cuisine. And that is
how we approach travel. When we eat while traveling
abroad, we instantly start to imagine how we'd introduce
those flavors at home. These dishes are internationally
inspired and tweaked to cook on our favorite
heat source: the grill.

We make no claims about authenticity. There are plenty of
people more qualified to carry that torch. Our only claim
is that these recipes are delicious. And we love them.
And our families love them.

CHICKEN CACCIATORE *Me If You Can*

Serves: 6 to 8 | Prep Time: 5 to 24 hours | Cook Time: 45 minutes

Smoky, charred grilled chicken and roasted veggies add welcomed layers to this braised dish. Make a double batch on a Sunday because this makes for some epic leftovers. Also, we have the seasoning for the chicken measured out here, but when we make this at home, we use our Italian dry brine. We sell it on our website with our partner Spiceology.

For the Chicken

1 (3- to 4-lb [1.4- to 1.8-kg]) chicken leg quarters, about 8 pieces

Kosher salt, for seasoning

½ tsp dried thyme

¼ tsp cayenne pepper

1 tbsp (15 ml) olive oil

For the Braise

3 tbsp (45 ml) olive oil

3 large red bell peppers, cut into strips

1 large sweet onion, cut into strips

6 cloves garlic, smashed

4 oz (113 g) cherry tomatoes

1 tsp kosher salt

½ cup (120 ml) dry white wine, such as sauvignon blanc or pinot grigio

1 (28-oz [794-kg]) can crushed tomatoes

3 tbsp (25 g) capers

4 stems fresh thyme

4 sprigs fresh oregano

½ tsp red pepper flakes

Pat the chicken pieces dry with paper towels and arrange them on a wire cooling rack set inside a rimmed baking sheet. Season generously with kosher salt, followed by the thyme and cayenne. Refrigerate the chicken, uncovered, for at least 4 hours or overnight.

Heat a gas grill to medium-high heat or prepare a charcoal grill for two-zone grilling. While the oven preheats, bring the chicken out of the fridge to take the chill off.

For the braise, drizzle a rimmed baking sheet or roasting pan with the olive oil. Add the red peppers, onion, garlic and tomatoes, and season with the kosher salt. Use tongs to toss the vegetables in the olive oil. Set the baking sheet on the grill and cook for 10 minutes, or until the tomatoes have burst, and the onion and red bell peppers are beginning to brown.

While the vegetables are browning, grill the chicken pieces. Coat the chicken pieces with the tablespoon (15 ml) of olive oil. Set the pieces, skin side down, over direct heat on the grill and cook until the skin begins to blacken, about 6 minutes per side. You can grill the chicken pieces alongside the vegetables, just try to keep the lid closed between adding and flipping the chicken.

When the chicken and vegetables are browned (they won't be cooked through yet), remove both from the grill. (Pro tip: You can set the chicken pieces on top of the vegetables to move them off the grill without dirtying another plate or pan.) Move the chicken pieces to a large Dutch oven (or oven-safe pot) and pour the vegetables over the chicken. Pour the wine onto the baking sheet to help loosen any stuck-on vegetable bits and then add this, along with the crushed tomatoes and capers to the Dutch oven. Gently stir to combine the chicken with the sauce. Add the thyme, oregano and red pepper flakes to the Dutch oven, add the lid and set the whole thing in the grill. Cook the cacciatore on the grill, covered, for 25 minutes. Remove the lid from the Dutch oven and cook for an additional 10 minutes, or until the sauce has thickened.

Remove the herb stems from the stew and serve the stew with the chicken pieces.

Korean BBQ BEEF RIBS

Serves: 4 to 6 | Prep Time: 2 hours | Cook Time: 6 to 6½ hours

We don't make traditional low-and-slow BBQ that often. But when we do, beef short ribs always top the list. It's clearly the supreme barbecued beef. Sorry about that overrated brisket. This dish is beefy, smoky, spicy, acidic, rich, salty and earthy. All that fancy talk really means is that it is delicious. And don't get trigger happy on the bulgogi sauce. If you start too early the sugar will burn and turn the whole dish into a bitter disgrace. And let's face it, your reputation with the in-laws might not survive another one.

For the Ribs

1 full plate bone-in beef short ribs, 5–6 lb (2.3–2.9 kg)

Kosher salt, for seasoning

Black pepper, for seasoning

1 tbsp (7 g) Sichuan chile powder

1 tbsp (7 g) smoked paprika

1 cup (240 ml) Korean bulgogi sauce

1 bunch scallions, sliced (see Tip)

For the Gochujang Mayo

½ cup (120 ml) mayo, we like Kewpie here

1 tbsp (15 ml) gochujang sauce

2 cloves garlic, grated

¼ cup (4 g) finely chopped fresh cilantro

1 tbsp (15 ml) lime juice, plus more if needed

Kosher salt, for seasoning

Pat the beef ribs dry with paper towels and season generously with kosher salt and black pepper. Sprinkle on the chile powder and smoked paprika. Set at room temperature for 1 hour and 59 minutes before smoking.

Heat the smoker to low heat, about 250°F (120°C) with cherry wood for smoking. We're going to get these ribs to an internal temperature of 190°F (88°C) before we begin basting. This will take 4 to 5 hours. When your ribs hit 190°F (88°C), begin basting them with the bulgogi sauce every 10 minutes until they reach 200 to 207°F (95 to 97°C), another 60 to 90 minutes.

Remove the ribs from the grill, cool for 20 minutes, then wrap them tightly in butcher paper and let them rest for 1 hour. While the ribs rest, make the Gochujang Mayo. In a medium mixing bowl, whisk together the mayo, gochujang, garlic, cilantro and lime juice, plus a pinch of kosher salt. Taste and add more lime juice or salt if needed.

Slice the beef into individual ribs and serve with the Gochujang Mayo and scallions.

JUST THE TIP:
For some dishes, we like to thinly slice the scallions lengthwise rather than on the bias for garnishing. If you throw these green onions strands in ice water, they'll curl up, making a pretty fucking cool garnish.

Mexican STREET CORN SALAD

Serves: 4 | Prep Time: 15 minutes | Cook Time: 25 minutes

This second-date–friendly version of a grilled corn salad takes some notes from our two favorite ways to eat corn . . . elote and esquites, which drops the mayo and adds salad stuff (see Mom, we do eat salad).

The charred, nutty corn combined with the bright, acidic and slightly sweet dressing and the salty, rich cotija makes for an epic side. If you have any vegetarians heading to the cookout, they will love you forever for making this.

For the Salad

4 ears fresh corn

2 tbsp (30 ml) olive oil

Kosher salt, for seasoning

1 small red onion, finely diced

4 oz (113 g) crumbled cotija cheese

2 cups (488 g) cherry tomatoes, halved or quartered

For the Cilantro Lime Vinaigrette

½ cup (120 ml) olive oil

¼ cup (60 ml) champagne vinegar

2 medium limes, washed and dried

2 tbsp (30 ml) honey

1 cup (16 g) fresh cilantro leaves

Kosher salt, for seasoning

Black pepper, for seasoning

Heat the grill for high direct heat. Husk the corn and coat each ear with the olive oil. Season well with kosher salt. Cook the corn directly on the grates, turning frequently until all the sides are charred, about 10 minutes total. Remove the corn from the grill to cool while you prepare the rest of the salad.

Make the vinaigrette by combining the olive oil and vinegar in a food processor or blender. Zest the limes directly into the oil mixture. Slice the limes in half and juice into the food processor as well, then add the honey, cilantro and a big pinch of kosher salt and black pepper. Pulse to combine. Taste and adjust the salt as needed.

Move half of the vinaigrette to a large serving bowl. Add the onion and let this marinate while you cut the kernels off the corn. Add the corn, cotija and tomatoes to the mixing bowl, and toss to combine. Taste and add more dressing, kosher salt and black pepper to your liking. Leftover dressing can be stored in the fridge for up to 3 days.

YOU'RE MY BABA GANOUSH
with Quick Grilled Flatbread

Serves: 6 to 8 | Prep Time: 30 minutes | Cook Time: 50 minutes

Baba ganoush is an earthy, creamy delight. An appetizer preceding a beautiful Mediterranean meal. Or pack some for lunch or a midday snack. It's perfect for dipping carrots, pita, even pretzels!

For the Baba Ganoush

2 lb (907 g) Japanese eggplant

1 head garlic

½ cup plus 2 tbsp (150 ml) olive oil, divided, plus more for seasoning

Kosher salt, for seasoning

1 tsp sumac, plus more for seasoning

1 tsp smoked paprika

2 tbsp (30 ml) fresh lemon juice

For the Quick Grilled Flatbread

1½ cups (208 g) self-rising flour, plus more for kneading and rolling

1½ cups (360 ml) plain whole milk Greek yogurt

2 tbsp (30 ml) olive oil

Kosher salt, for seasoning

1 tsp sumac

1 cup (60 g) mixed fresh herbs, we love parsley and mint

Heat the smoker to medium heat, about 300°F (150°C). Split the eggplants in half lengthwise, cut off the top of the head of garlic, coat the eggplant and garlic with the 2 tablespoons (30 ml) of olive oil. Season everything generously with kosher salt. Add the eggplant to the smoker, cut side up, along with the garlic. Smoke until both the garlic and eggplant are buttery tender, about 25 minutes. While the eggplant cooks, prepare the flatbread.

In a large mixing bowl, beat together the self-rising flour and yogurt. The dough will be shaggy but should come together into a loose mound. Dust a work surface with additional flour and dump the dough out onto it. Knead the dough, folding it over onto itself until smooth. Round into a uniform ball and cover loosely with plastic wrap. Rest the dough for 15 minutes. Remove the eggplant and garlic from the grill, and cool while you roll and grill the flatbread.

Divide the yogurt dough into four pieces and roughly roll each piece out into a round-ish oval—you're going to tear the finished flatbread into pieces for dipping, so don't stress about perfect rounds. Brush the dough with the olive oil and grill on the smoker until charred and puffed, about 4 minutes per side. Remove from the grill, and sprinkle with kosher salt and the sumac.

When the eggplant is cool enough to handle, scoop out the tender flesh into a food processor, and do the same with the roasted garlic. Add the sumac, smoked paprika and a pinch of kosher salt. Process until smooth. Stop, scrape down the food processor bowl with a spatula, return the lid and process again. With the machine running, slowly drizzle in the ½ cup (120 ml) of olive oil and the lemon juice. You can add a few tablespoons (30 ml) of water if needed to emulsify. Taste and season the dip with more salt, if needed. Serve the baba ganoush with a drizzle of olive oil, sprinkle of sumac and lots of herbs on top, alongside the torn flatbread for dipping.

JUST THE TIP:
No self-rising flour? No problem. Just add 1 tablespoon (14 g) baking powder and 1 teaspoon kosher salt to 1½ cups (188 g) all-purpose flour for this dough.

Patatas Bravas POUTINE

Serves: 6 to 8 | Prep Time: 60 minutes | Cook Time: 75 minutes

We're not sure if Spain and Canada are going to be okay with us combining their national potato dishes. But chances are they won't ever read this cookbook, so we'll roll the dice. And when you take your first bite of this smoky, crispy, sausage-and-cheese-topped potato masterpiece, you'll know why we took our chances.

For the Potatoes

3 lb (1.4 kg) Yukon gold potatoes

Kosher salt, for seasoning

2 tsp (4 g) hot smoked paprika

2 tbsp (30 ml) olive oil

8 oz (226 g) Spanish chorizo links, halved and sliced into half-moons

For the Garlic Aioli

½ cup (120 ml) mayo

2 tbsp (30 ml) lemon juice

2 cloves garlic, finely grated on a box grater

For the Salsa Bravas

1 small yellow onion, thinly sliced

2 tsp (4 g) hot smoked paprika

½ tsp kosher salt

½ tsp cayenne pepper

2 tbsp (30 ml) olive oil

3 cloves garlic, minced

1 (14-oz [397-g]) can diced tomatoes

2 tbsp (30 ml) sherry vinegar

For Serving

1½ cups (170 g) Cheddar cheese curds

¼ cup (12 g) finely chopped chives

Peel your potatoes and cut them into ½ inch (1.3 cm) pieces. Bring a large pot of water to a boil over medium-high heat. Season heavily with salt and add the potatoes. Cook the potatoes until tender, about 5 minutes. Drain the potatoes and spread out to cool on a paper towel–lined baking sheet. While the potatoes cool, make the Garlic Aioli and the Salsa Bravas.

In a small bowl, combine the mayo, lemon juice and grated garlic. Whisk until smooth and chill until ready to serve.

Heat the grill to medium heat. In a small bowl, toss the onion with the paprika, salt, cayenne and olive oil to coat. Grill the onion until it's just beginning to char and soften, 6 to 8 minutes. Remove from the grill and cool for 5 minutes. Move the onion and any juices to a blender or food processor. Add the garlic, tomatoes in their juices and the sherry vinegar. Blend the Salsa Bravas until smooth. Set aside.

Heat the grill to medium-high, aiming for a temp between 400 to 450°F (205 to 230°C). Toss the cooled potatoes with more kosher salt and smoked paprika. Add the olive oil and toss to coat. Spread the potatoes in an even layer on a rimmed baking sheet. Cook the potatoes on the grill, with the lid closed, for 15 minutes. Use a thin spatula to flip the potatoes (if there's lots of sticking, close the grill for 5 minutes and try again), and then add the chorizo to the pan. Cook for another 15 to 20 minutes, until the potatoes are crispy.

To serve, pile some potatoes and chorizo into a serving bowl. Add the Salsa Bravas, followed by the cheese curds and then a drizzle of aioli, finishing the bowl with chopped chives.

JUST THE TIP:

Magic happens when you cook potatoes twice. You get a crispy, golden outside and soft, pillowy inside. We're going to skip the fryer and achieve this by parboiling them then roasting them in the grill. Crispy potatoes are better when the house doesn't smell like the deep fryer for 3 days.

Rolled Up and Smoked MANICOTTI

Serves: 4 to 5 | Prep Time: 60 minutes | Cook Time: 30 minutes

The manicotti we know is more Italian American than Italian. So much so that it probably doesn't belong in this section. Sorry, Italy. One thing that was always missing from this dish was layers of flavor and texture. The grilled sausage brings some smoky Maillard reaction and the pancetta brings a nice salty crunch. Spring for the fancy local ricotta. It's the backbone of the dish.

1 lb (454 g) spicy Italian sausage

1 batch Sheet-Pan Red Sauce (page 83)

4 oz (113 g) pancetta, cubed

1 (15- to 16-oz [425- to 454-g]) container full-fat ricotta cheese

2 cups (224 g) shredded part-skim mozzarella cheese, divided

½ cup (50 g) finely grated Parmesan cheese, divided

½ cup (30 g) chopped fresh parsley leaves, divided

1 large egg, lightly beaten

1 tbsp (6 g) lemon zest

Kosher salt, for seasoning

1 (8-oz [226-g]) box dried manicotti pasta tubes, about 14 tubes

2 tbsp (30 ml) olive oil

Heat the grill for high direct heat. Add the sausage directly to the grill and cook, until charred and cooked through, turning occasionally, about 8 minutes total. If you're making the Sheet-Pan Red Sauce, reduce the heat on the grill and cook the sauce ingredients while you prepare the filling and cook the pasta.

Crisp the pancetta in a small skillet over medium heat. Drain on paper towels. Roughly chop the grilled sausage. Dump the ricotta into a large mixing bowl and add ½ of the mozzarella, ½ of the Parmesan and ½ of the parsley. Add the egg and lemon zest, and season liberally with kosher salt. Mix until well combined, and then add the sausage and pancetta. Chill while you cook the pasta.

Bring a large pot of water to boil. Salt heavily, like we're talking about seawater heavy, and add the manicotti shells. Cook until al dente—about 8 minutes, but check your pasta box for guidelines. Drain the manicotti and spread it into an even layer on a baking sheet to cool.

Move the chilled filling to a large zip-top bag. Seal the bag and then cut a 1-inch (2.5-cm) piece off of one of the corners. Put on some Marvin Gaye and slowly pipe some filling into each of the cooked manicotti shells. Subtle moans would be appropriate. A pro tip is to pipe the filling into both ends, rather than trying to force the filling into one end all the way through—you'll end up with fewer broken shells this way too.

You can bake this manicotti in a 9 x 13–inch (23 x 33–cm) baking dish, but we like to serve these stuffed pasta shells in three to four shell portions baked in small cast-iron skillets (four to five of them). Here's how we build them. Coat your baking dish(es) of choice with the olive oil. Spoon about ½ cup (120 ml) of the Sheet-Pan Red Sauce into each dish. Add three to four manicotti depending on the size of your skillets and top with another ½ cup (120 ml) of the Sheet-Pan Red Sauce. Casserolers, you'll want to put ⅔ of your sauce in the pan first before adding all the shells and topping with the remaining sauce. Sprinkle the manicotti with the remaining mozzarella and Parmesan cheeses.

Set the grill to medium-high heat for indirect cooking. Return the assembled manicotti to the grill and cook for 30 minutes, until the cheese and sauce is bubbly and beginning to brown. Top the finished casserole with the remaining parsley and serve hot.

SCHNITZEL, *I Don't Even Know Her*

Serves: 4 | Prep Time: 60 minutes | Cook Time: 45 minutes

Schnitzel is on the Mt. Rushmore of magical crispy cutlets alongside the Italian milanese and Japanese katsu. The brilliance of schnitzel is the restraint and simplicity. It can stand alone; however, when finished with a touch of a creamy mustard sauce and fresh lemon juice, you get heaven. It may be the perfect food.

For the love of God, don't do this in your air fryer.

Caution Note: Frying on the grill is very dangerous. Make sure to read our safety notes on page 15 before proceeding. Have a nice day.

For the Schnitzel

4 boneless pork loin chops, about 4–5 oz (113–142 g) each, thinner is better

Kosher salt, for seasoning

1 cup (108 g) unseasoned breadcrumbs

1 cup (56 g) panko breadcrumbs

1 cup (125 g) all-purpose flour

4 large eggs

1 qt (960 ml) oil, for frying

1 lemon, cut into wedges

For the Mustard Cream Sauce

¾ cup (180 ml) heavy cream

¼ cup (60 ml) sour cream

3 tbsp (45 ml) Dijon mustard

1 tbsp (2 g) fresh thyme leaves

Kosher salt, for seasoning

Black pepper, for seasoning

Working with one chop at a time, pound the pork chops with the tenderizing side of a meat mallet to double the size. Season the hell out of the pork chops with kosher salt. Set aside while you set up for breading the chops.

Combine the breadcrumbs and panko in a food processor, and process to a fine crumb. Set up a breading station using three shallow dishes. Fill the first with the all-purpose flour, seasoned with a pinch of kosher salt. Fill the second with the eggs, lightly beaten with a fork and seasoned with a pinch of kosher salt. Fill the third with the fine breadcrumbs, and you guessed it—a pinch of kosher salt. Coat each of the pork chops by pressing into the flour, dipping in the egg (make sure both sides get good coverage), and then really press the chops into the breadcrumb mixture to coat. Set the chops aside on a cooling rack—air circulation will help the breading set while you get ready for frying.

Frying on the grill can be dangerous, so set yourself up for success by having all your tools nearby: a deep Dutch oven is great for frying, a clean kitchen towel, a cooling rack set inside a rimmed baking sheet for the finished schnitzel, a thermometer, tongs, kosher salt and a cold beer (x2) are all helpful.

To make the cream sauce, heat the heavy cream and sour cream in a small saucepan over direct heat. Bring this mixture to a simmer, whisking until thickened, about 6 minutes. Add the mustard and thyme, season with a pinch each of kosher salt and black pepper, and cook for 2 minutes. Move off the grill or keep over direct heat to keep warm while you fry the schnitzel.

Heat the grill for two-zone cooking with the heated side on high. Heat the oil in a Dutch oven to 375°F (190°C) on the heated side of the grill. Add the schnitzel pieces one at a time, and deep-fry until golden and crispy, about 3 minutes each. Carefully remove the schnitzel to the cooling rig set on the indirect side. Season with kosher salt immediately after frying.

Serve the schnitzel with the warm cream sauce and lemon wedges.

THINGS WE EAT THAT ARE

NOT MEAT

(But Don't Worry There's More Meat)

We know what you might be thinking . . . The Grill Dads only cook meat on grills. Well, that couldn't be further from the truth. In fact, you might be surprised to know that we cook as many fruits and veggies on the grill as we do meat. Don't believe us? Just wait until you see the recipes in this chapter.

We've traveled all over the world and have come to learn that vegetables play a major role right next to the meat. Or, in many cases, as a perfectly delicious substitute. No longer will the humble carrot have to take a back seat to other things made on the grill. The bashful cabbage can come out from the shadows and stand tall. The red pepper can flex its majesty and offer the world something so incredible that it'll have meat shaking in its boots.

OK, so that might be a bit dramatic, but what we mean to say is that veggies and fruits have every right to adorn a grill alongside meat and, in some instances, stand alone. In fact, there is no better way to prepare a veggie than on the grill.

So, sit back, relax and get ready to throw down with our inventive and fun NOT MEAT recipes. Enjoy.

CABBAGE WITH YOGURT SAUCE

Serves: 6 to 8 | Prep Time: 40 minutes | Cook Time: 70 minutes

A few years back we had the privilege of eating at an amazing restaurant called Charcoal Venice located in Venice, California. Created by two-star Michelin chef Josiah Citrin, Charcoal Venice is a restaurant that was inspired by family backyard barbecues. Inside the kitchen, Josiah uses the Big Green Eggs to cook some of the most interesting and tasty food we've eaten. It is with this inspiration and homage that we are excited to share this grilled cabbage with yogurt sauce recipe.

We recommend serving this with Schnitzel, I Don't Even Know Her (page 109).

1 large head green cabbage

2 tbsp (30 ml) olive oil, plus more for serving

Kosher salt, for seasoning

1 cup (240 ml) whole milk Greek yogurt

3 tbsp (45 ml) lemon juice

2 cloves garlic, grated

1 tsp ground turmeric

½ tsp ground cumin

Black pepper, for seasoning

Heat one charcoal chimney worth of lump charcoal to white ashy hot—this will take about 40 minutes. Coat the head of cabbage with the olive oil and season it seriously with kosher salt. Dump the lit charcoal into your charcoal grill. Use a charcoal rack or tongs to make a hole in the middle of the charcoal and set the whole head of cabbage inside of it. Yup, we're going to char the whole head. Push some of the hot coals around the cabbage, and cook until the entire head of cabbage is black and a probe or skewer slides in like butter, about 1 hour. You can even set a grate over the cabbage and cook something else while it chars, like our The Very Best Grilled Chicken Ever (page 50).

While the cabbage roasts, whisk together the yogurt, lemon juice, garlic, turmeric and cumin in a medium bowl. Season to taste with salt and black pepper, and chill until the cabbage is ready.

When the cabbage is tender, remove it from the grill and cool for about 10 minutes. Then, use a large knife to cut it into quarters. Use the knife to cut the core off each piece, and season the cabbage with more salt and a drizzle of oil. We like to serve the cabbage with the charred leaves plated underneath—they aren't tasty, but still pretty fucking cool as a decoration—and the yogurt sauce for dipping.

JUST THE TIP:

This recipe can also be done in a gas grill or smoker, set inside a cast-iron skillet. Crank the grill to high and cook until the cabbage is charred, 40 to 50 minutes.

Roasty and Toasty GAZPACHO

Serves: 6 | Prep Time: 15 minutes | Cook Time: 25 minutes

Inspired by our many trips to Spain, we decided to put a bit of a grilling twist on a traditional Spanish gazpacho recipe. Using a grill to roast the tomatoes, onion and peppers gives them that smoky and earthy flavor that pairs perfectly with the acid from the vinegar. And for our money, it doesn't get much better than eating this soup with a grilled piece of baguette.

This one could be a meal on its own or a perfect partner with Good Mojo Picón Flank Steak (page 24).

3 lb (1.4 kg) ripe Roma tomatoes

2 large red bell peppers

½ cup plus 2 tbsp (150 ml) olive oil, divided, plus more for finishing

Kosher salt, for seasoning

1 medium red onion, roughly chopped

4 cloves garlic, grated

3 tbsp (45 ml) red wine vinegar

1 large fresh baguette, divided

Flaky salt, for serving

1 small bunch parsley, finely chopped

Sour cream, for serving

Heat the grill for medium-high direct heat. Halve the tomatoes and remove the pulpy core. Coat the tomatoes and bell peppers with 1 tablespoon (15 ml) of the olive oil and season with kosher salt. Grill the tomatoes and bell peppers directly on the grill grates until the tomatoes are softened and the bell peppers are charred, about 10 minutes. Remove the vegetables to a large mixing bowl and set aside to cool.

Build the rest of the gazpacho in a blender while the veggies cool. Combine the red onion, garlic and red wine vinegar in the blender. Tear off half of the baguette and rip it into bite-sized pieces, then add these to the blender. Add the tomatoes. Remove the blackened skin and seeds from the bell peppers, then add the bell peppers to the blender as well. Puree the gazpacho until smooth, stop, scrape down the sides of the blender and puree again. This time, stream in ½ cup (120 ml) of the olive oil while you blend the soup. Move the blender to the fridge to chill while you grill the rest of the baguette for serving.

Slice the remaining baguette on the bias and brush with the remaining 1 tablespoon (15 ml) of olive oil. Grill the bread until toasty, 1 to 2 minutes per side. Serve the gazpacho with a drizzle of olive oil, flaky salt, parsley and a dollop of sour cream. The grilled bread is dope for dunking.

ROASTED RED PEPPER FARRO,

Is It Me You're Looking for Salad

Serves: 4 to 6 | Prep Time: 20 minutes | Cook Time: 35 minutes

Farro is an old Italian grain that if you haven't tried it yet, run, don't walk, to the grocery store and pick some up. Farro has a nutty, earthy and subtly sweet flavor that makes this ancient grain one of the most incredible choices for this salad. Combined with the smoky charred peppers, fresh tomato, raw shallots and sharp champagne vinegar, this salad will make you a culinary hero at your next gathering.
Time to put your cape on . . .

Serve this one with our Tuscan Tomahawk with Impressively Huge Bone (page 34).

4 large red bell peppers

Kosher salt, for seasoning

2 cups (about 10 oz [283 g]) dried farro

1 medium shallot

4 cloves garlic

3 tbsp (45 ml) champagne vinegar

¼ cup (60 ml) olive oil

1 pint (298 g) cherry tomatoes, halved

1 cup (60 g) fresh parsley leaves

Heat the grill for direct medium-high heat. Wash and dry the bell peppers. Set the bell peppers directly onto the grill and turn them every 2 to 3 minutes until they are deeply charred and wrinkling. Remove the bell peppers to a bowl and top with plastic wrap or a pot lid. Set aside for 5 minutes.

While the bell peppers cool, cook the farro. Bring a medium pot of water to a boil over medium-high heat. Season heavily with salt and add the farro. Cook until tender, about 15 minutes. Drain the farro and season with a pinch of kosher salt while hot.

Peel the charred skin from the bell peppers, and remove and discard their seeds. Reserve half of one bell pepper for the salad. Add the red bell peppers, shallot, garlic and champagne vinegar to a blender or food processor. Pulse to combine, and then add the olive oil and a hefty pinch of kosher salt. Process again until you have a smooth, thin dressing.

Add half of the dressing to the farro. Chop the reserved bell pepper and add to the farro salad. Add the tomatoes and parsley. Taste and season with more salt or more dressing. Serve this salad slightly warm, at room temp or cold.

COUSCOUS COUSCOUS SALAD
(It's So Good We Say It Twice Twice)

Serves: 6 to 8 | Prep Time: 30 minutes | Cook Time: 25 minutes

The simplicity and flavor fullness that comes with using tricolor pearl couscous alongside the nutty and semi-sweet flavor of feta cheese, and the earthy sweetness of heirloom tomatoes will make this Mediterranean-inspired salad a super special standout.

We love this one as a side to our Little Red Bavette with Real Herby Chimichurri (page 27).

3 cups (720 ml) chicken broth

2 cups (300 g) uncooked tricolor pearl couscous

Kosher salt, for seasoning

1 (8-oz [226-g]) block feta cheese

1 medium onion, cut into disks

¼ cup plus 2 tbsp (90 ml) olive oil, divided

1 large English cucumber

2 large heirloom or beefsteak tomatoes

1 medium lemon, washed and dried

¼ cup (23 g) finely chopped fresh mint

Bring the chicken broth to a boil over medium-high heat in a medium saucepan. Stir in the couscous and cover. Cook for 8 to 10 minutes or until the couscous is tender. Pearl couscous will absorb most of the broth, but drain off any excess (you can save this for another use). Move the couscous to a large bowl and season with a big pinch of kosher salt.

Heat the grill for medium-high indirect cooking. Brush the block of feta and the onion disks with the 2 tablespoons (30 ml) of olive oil, and season the shit out of them with kosher salt. Grill the onion disks over direct heat until charred, about 4 minutes per side, and then move to the unheated side of the grill to soften. Put the block of feta directly on the grill grates and cook until lightly browned, about 2 minutes. Remove the feta—a fish spatula is best for this—and onion and set aside while you prepare the rest of the salad.

Cut the English cucumber into quarters lengthwise, and then chop into ¼-inch (6-mm) wedges. Roughly chop the tomatoes and the grilled onion. Add all the chopped veggies to the still warm couscous and stir to combine. Season again with a pinch of kosher salt. Dress the salad with the remaining olive oil, the zest and juice of the lemon, and the chopped mint. Taste and adjust the seasoning before crumbling the feta over the salad. Serve this salad warm or at room temperature.

Ouch.

Grilled POTATO SALAD

Serves: 4 to 6 | Prep Time: 15 minutes | Cook Time: 30 minutes

This isn't your grandma's mayo-drenched potato salad. And although we don't have anything against your grandma, we think this recipe would put a smackdown on her. Hi, Gramma!

Grilling the potatoes for this recipe gives this tired picnic staple a smoky smack in the potato ass. Combine those smoky spuds with some cubed-up pancetta, and you've got a winner at the county fair.

Guys - potatoes don't have asses

This is the dish that is best served with Pinkies Up Smashburger (page 137).

8 oz (226 g) cubed pancetta

1½ lb (680 g) small Yukon gold potatoes, halved lengthwise

Kosher salt, for seasoning

3 tbsp (45 ml) olive oil

½ cup (120 ml) mayo

¼ cup (60 ml) sour cream

2 tbsp (30 ml) Dijon mustard

2 hard-boiled eggs, chopped

2 bunches chives, chopped

Heat the grill to medium-high. Place a cold cast-iron skillet on the grill and add the pancetta. Let the pan and pancetta slowly heat up together, and then cook the pancetta to crisp, stirring regularly, about 15 minutes. Spoon the pancetta from the pan to a paper towel–lined plate. Toss the potatoes with pancetta fat directly in the pan (tongs work well for this) and season with a pinch of kosher salt.

Move the potatoes from the pan directly onto the grill grates. Grill for 8 to 10 minutes, or until nicely charred, then flip. Grill until the potatoes are tender, another 10 to 12 minutes.

Remove the potatoes to a small bowl and toss with the olive oil. Cool the potatoes for 5 minutes. While the potatoes cool, whisk together the mayo, sour cream, mustard and a pinch of kosher salt in a large bowl. Add the pancetta and potatoes, and toss to coat. Finish the potato salad with the chopped eggs and chives.

Miso My SHISHITO

We really just included this recipe because it's fun to say "shishito." Hahaha. Right? Right! Anyway, we love shishito peppers and we love artichokes. So, grilling them and putting them together adds an exxxtra special twist to two of the world's tastiest veggies.

But the real reason we're making both is because we need as many things as possible to dip in the miso mayo sauce. It's a damn symphony in your mouth. Don't believe us? You will. Oh yes, you will.

These make a great snack, or even dinner when paired with our Mark's BBQ Oysters with West Carolina Mignonette (page 174).

For the Veggies

8 baby artichokes

1 large lemon, halved

1 lb (454 g) shishito peppers

Kosher salt, for seasoning

For the Miso Mayo Sauce

2 tbsp (30 g) white miso

2 tsp (10 ml) rice wine vinegar

1 cup (240 ml) mayo

1 bunch chives, finely chopped

½ cup (8 g) finely chopped cilantro

Kosher salt, for seasoning

Prep the baby artichokes by peeling off the dark green outer leaves and trimming any sharp tips. Cut off the top one-quarter of the artichoke leaves, so you've got just the pale tender leaves. Quarter the artichokes and rub them with ½ of the cut lemon.

Make the Miso Mayo Sauce by whisking together the miso and vinegar in a medium bowl. This helps break up the thick miso paste. Add the mayo, chives and cilantro, and season with a pinch of kosher salt.

Heat the grill to medium-high. Spread the artichokes on a rimmed baking sheet, add 1 cup (240 ml) of water, squeeze out the juice of the remaining ½ of the lemon, and cover with aluminum foil. Steam the artichokes for 10 minutes, or until tender.

Remove the baking sheet from the grill and move the artichokes from the steamer sheet and pat dry. Season the artichokes and the shishitos with a pinch of kosher salt.

Return the artichokes to the grill, this time directly on the grates. Add the shishitos and cook both vegetables until charred and tender, about 10 times, flipping as needed for even color.

Serve the grilled artichokes and shishitos with the Miso Mayo Sauce.

ROASTED CALI-FLOWER *with Chive Oil*

Serves: 4, makes about 1 cup (240 ml) Chive Oil | Prep Time: 30 minutes | Cook Time: 45 minutes

Cauliflower is one of our favorite veggies to grill. It's hearty, holds up and you can either throw a head of cauliflower into the coals, grill on the grates or even smoke it. It's all up to you. But the real twist on this recipe is to make our baller Chive Oil— something that you'll probably drink with a straw. It's so damn good.

This dish has to go with our Chicken Paillard So Thin It Only Has One Side (page 60).

For the Chive Oil

5 bunches chives

1 cup (240 ml) vegetable oil

For the Cauliflower

1 large head cauliflower, about 2 lb (907 g)

¼ cup (60 ml) olive oil

Kosher salt, for seasoning

Black pepper, for seasoning

2 tsp (6 g) turmeric

1 tsp ground cumin

Flaky salt, for serving

First up, let's make some Chive Oil. Bring a large pot of water to a boil. Fill a bowl with water and ice. Boil the chives for 1 minute then plunge immediately into the ice water. Remove the chives from the ice bath and dry on a paper towel for about 10 minutes. Combine the oil and chives in a blender. Blend with the oil for a long-ass time, longer than you think, 3 to 5 minutes. Pour the chive oil through a fine strainer. We like to move the chive oil to a squeeze bottle for saving and serving.

Heat the grill to high. Set the whole head of cauliflower in a 10-inch (25-cm) skillet, drizzle with the olive oil and season with the kosher salt, black pepper, turmeric and cumin. Set the skillet on the grill, and cook the cauliflower until it is pretty aggressively charred and probe tender, 35 to 40 minutes.

Remove the cauliflower from the grill and slice it into eight wedges. Drizzle the cauliflower with the Chive Oil and season with flaky salt to serve.

VEGGIE TIP:
This oil will stay for a few weeks and works great on eggs, potatoes, steak or even a crusty baguette.

KNOW YOUR ROOTS
Maple Chile Turnips, Parsnips and Tri-Colored Carrots

Serves: 8 to 10 | Prep Time: 15 minutes | Cook Time: 45 minutes

One way to up your roasted root veggie game is to spice it up by adding chile peppers and sweet paprika, and then combining it with maple syrup to wrap that heat in sweetness. This is an all-time dinner table favorite at our houses that seldom results in leftovers. But if there are any, try making a root veggie pancake the next day and see what you think.

This trio of root vegetables pairs perfectly with the Not Your Grandma's Dry Turkey and Stuffing (page 63).

1 lb (454 g) turnips

1 lb (454 g) parsnips

1 lb (454 g) medium tri-colored carrots

¼ cup (60 ml) olive oil

Kosher salt, for seasoning

Black pepper, for seasoning

3 tbsp (45 g) maple sugar or maple syrup

2 tbsp (28 g) brown sugar

1 tsp chile pepper

1 tsp sweet paprika

4 oz (113 g; 1 stick) salted butter, cubed

Heat the grill for medium-high direct heat. Line a rimmed baking sheet with foil.

Rinse and scrub the turnips, parsnips and carrots. Cut the turnips into quarters. Peel the parsnips and carrots, and cut them on the bias into 1-inch (2.5-cm) pieces. Spread the vegetables onto the prepared baking sheet. Toss with the olive oil and season with kosher salt and black pepper.

Roast the root vegetables on the grill for 20 minutes until they are just beginning to brown. Toss the vegetables and then add the maple sugar, brown sugar, chile pepper, sweet paprika and the butter cubes. Cook for another 15 to 20 minutes, until the vegetables are deeply browned and caramelized.

A SHAMELESS PLUG FROM MARK AND FEY:
Yup, this spice mixture is based on our maple chili blend, which you can swap in here. We swap out the chile pepper for crushed red pepper, ancho, chipotle or whatever we have on hand.

ROASTED BROCCOLINI *with Chiles*

Serves: 4 | Prep Time: 10 minutes | Cook Time: 25 minutes

This recipe is definitely an homage to a classic Italian dish, but we put a slight twist on it by grilling the broccolini after blanching. And the great thing about this dish is you can add as much or as little heat to fit you or your guests' preferences. It's the simplicity of this dish that truly lets the veggie shine in all its grilled glory!

This veggie dish pairs wonderfully with our Itty Bitty Chickie Committee Chicken Roulades (page 70).

Kosher salt, for seasoning

2 bunches broccolini, about 8 oz (226 g)

1 tbsp (15 ml) olive oil

Black pepper, for seasoning

1 lemon, washed and dried

2 small Fresno chiles, thinly sliced

Flaky salt, for serving

Bring a large pot of water to a boil over medium-high heat. Fill a large bowl with ice and cold water. Season the boiling water well with salt, we're talking sea-level salinity here. Add the broccolini and cook for 2 minutes, then immediately plunge the broccolini into the ice bath. Chill for 5 minutes and drain.

Heat the grill for high direct heat. Toss the broccolini in the olive oil, kosher salt and black pepper. Add the pieces directly to the grill and cook until charred, about 2 minutes. Flip the broccolini and continue to cook for 2 minutes more. Remove the broccolini from the grill, and season with the zest of a lemon and ½ its juice, then add the chiles and a sprinkle of flaky salt. Serve hot.

DOWN THE HATCH CHILE *Au Gratin*

Serves: 4 | Prep Time: 40 minutes | Cook Time: 60 to 75 minutes

You know what's great about hatch chiles? Freaking everything. Hatch chiles are one of the most versatile and amazing peppers to use in just about any recipe. A native of New Mexico, hatch chiles have a short season of harvest and are one of the most sought-after peppers you can get. From salsas and soups to sauces and sides, hatch chiles are the gold nuggets of the pepper planet. They are more green than gold, but you get the point. Check our recipe for a super smoky and savory twist on potatoes au gratin.

This cheesy potato-ey wonder is great served with our
Fancy Pants Ribeye Roast Beef (page 42).

4 large hatch chiles

4 tbsp (56 g) salted butter

¼ cup (31 g) all-purpose flour

3 cups (720 ml) heavy cream

4 oz (113 g) cream cheese

1 cup (113 g) shredded sharp Cheddar cheese, divided

1 cup (113 g) shredded Monterey Jack cheese, divided

Kosher salt, for seasoning

4 large russet potatoes, about 3 lb (1.4 kg)

1 small yellow onion

4 cloves garlic, minced

Heat the grill for high direct heat. Add the chiles directly to the grill and cook until blackened, turning twice, about 10 minutes total time. Move the chiles to a bowl, and cover with plastic wrap or a lid to steam and cool.

Heat the butter in a medium saucepan on the stovetop over medium heat. Add the flour and cook until the roux smells like pancakes and looks dry, about 3 minutes. Add the heavy cream and whisk vigorously to smooth. Bring the sauce to a bubbling simmer and cook until thickened, about 5 minutes more. Remove the sauce from the heat and whisk in the cream cheese, ½ the Cheddar and ½ the Monterey Jack. Taste the sauce and season with kosher salt.

Use a mandoline to thinly slice the potatoes and onion. Remove the skin and seeds from the chile peppers, and roughly chop the them.

Pour ⅓ of the cheese sauce into a 9 x 13–inch (23 x 33–cm) casserole dish. Layer the potatoes, onion, garlic and ½ of the hatch chiles. Top with the remaining cheese sauce, then sprinkle on the remaining Cheddar and Monterey Jack cheese and the chiles. Cover the casserole with foil.

Reduce the heat of the grill to medium. Bake the au gratin on the grill, covered, for 40 minutes. Check that the potatoes are very tender and remove the foil. Cook until the cheese is brown, 10 to 12 minutes more.

Cool the au gratin for 15 minutes before slicing and serving.

LET'S MAKE SANDWICHES

HOAGIE'S HEROES

(Our Favorite Sandwich is the Next One)

There is a general rule that we live by:
If it is good, it is better in a sandwich.

And our definition of a sandwich is broad. For the sake of
this book, we'll say anything held together by two pieces
of bread, or bread-like product, constitutes a sandwich.

Hang on tight, because we're about to unleash some
legendary handheld culinary adventures.

Pinkies Up SMASHBURGER

Serves: 4 | Prep Time: 60 minutes | Cook Time: 25 minutes

Extravagant burgers don't need to be a half pound, cooked in a sous vide and sprinkled with edible gold flakes. In fact, fuck those burgers.

This is our favorite style of burger: the smashburger. High-end, highly marbled meat fried to a perfectly juicy burger in its own fat until the Maillard reaction nirvana is achieved with an epic crust. We suggest you grind your own beef for this. The tools are accessible, it's oddly satisfying and tastes much fresher. And for all you assholes on the internet that respond to this recipe with "stop squishing all the juices out," you don't deserve this burger.

For the Burger Patties

1 lb (454 g) high-fat ground beef, like chuck or highbrow Wagyu

Kosher salt, for seasoning

Black pepper, for seasoning

1 tsp garlic powder, divided

For the Spicy Aioli

1 cup (240 ml) mayo

2 cloves garlic, grated

1 tbsp (15 ml) Dijon mustard

1 tsp cayenne pepper

Kosher salt, for seasoning

Black pepper, for seasoning

For Serving

4 potato buns

4 slices thick-cut American cheese (thick-cut Boar's Head is so fucking good)

4 oz (113 g) watercress

Divide the beef into four rounds—not patties, but loose rounds to smash later. Place the rounds on a plate and loosely cover with foil. Chill the rounds in the fridge while you prep the sauce and grill.

While the beef chills, make the Spicy Aioli. Just whisk together the mayo, garlic, mustard and cayenne in a medium-sized bowl. Season with a pinch of kosher salt and black pepper too.

Heat the grill for direct, high-heat cooking. Toast the burger buns over high heat then set aside. Heat a large griddle or skillet over direct heat. Working in batches of two, add two beef rounds to the skillet at a time. Season each with a heavy pinch of kosher salt, black pepper and ¼ teaspoon of the garlic powder. Let the burgers go until some fat pools at the bottom of the burger. Use a large flat spatula to press down hard on each patty for 2 minutes. The burgers should be super thin and have a diameter that is at least 2 inches (5 cm) wider than the bun (if your pan is too small, you may only be able to do one at a time).

When the juices in the middle of the burger start to bubble up, flip the burgers. Wait 1 minute, then add the cheese. Remove the burgers after another 2 to 3 minutes, when the cheese is totally melted. Repeat with the remaining beef rounds and cheese.

Build the burgers with a swipe of Spicy Aioli on the buns and a burger patty topped with watercress on each. These can only be eaten with your pinkies up.

GRILLED, GRILLED CHEESE
with Pineapple Bacon Jam and Ham

Serves: 4, makes about 2 cups (480 ml) Pineapple Bacon Jam | Prep Time: 20 minutes | Cook Time: 15 minutes

Go figure. Grilled cheese is actually better when it is grilled. The bread is smoky and perfectly toasted; the cheese is sharp and smooth; and the jam is bright, salty and sweet with a kiss of heat. It has it all.

For the Pineapple Bacon Jam

1 lb (454 g) bacon, cut into ½-inch (1.3-cm) pieces

4 shallots, thinly sliced

1 (8-oz [226-g]) can crushed pineapple

½ cup (110 g) light brown sugar

⅓ cup (80 ml) apple cider vinegar

½ tsp red pepper flakes

For the Grilled Cheese Sammies

8 oz (226 g) thinly sliced ham

8 oz (226 g) shredded Provolone

8 oz (226 g) shredded sharp Cheddar

8 slices sourdough bread, about ½ inch (1.3 cm) thick

½ cup (120 ml) mayo

Kick things off here by making the Pineapple Bacon Jam. In a medium saucepan, cook the bacon until crisp, stirring regularly, about 10 minutes. Spoon off the crisp bacon (drain on a paper towel) and add the shallots to the bacon fat. Cook the shallots until softened, about 4 minutes, then add the pineapple, sugar, apple cider vinegar and red pepper flakes. Continue cooking the jam until the juices are reduced, the shallots and pineapple are browned and the mixture is, well, jammy, about 10 minutes. Stir in the bacon and set aside to cool.

Heat the grill for medium heat. Grill the ham for 2 minutes to heat through. Build the sandwiches by layering the bacon jam, ham and cheeses between 2 slices of bread. Coat the outside of each sandwich with mayo.

Cook the sandwiches directly on the grill. Move the sandwiches often to avoid charring the bread, and cook until the bread is golden brown and the cheese is melted, about 6 minutes.

McActually McGood RIB SANDWICH

Serves: 6 to 8 | Prep Time: 4 to 24 hours | Cook Time: 4 hours

The fast-food version of this sandwich is totally McFine. But it deserves to be McAmazing. This is not our attempt at a copycat. It is how we would make a rib sandwich at home. And when we think of a pork sandwich, we think banh mi. So, if you're looking for a recipe to make microwaved pork covered in ketchup and liquid smoke, keep movin'.

For the Ribs

2 (2-lb [907-g]) racks baby back ribs

Kosher salt, for seasoning

Black pepper, for seasoning

For the BBQ Sauce

⅓ cup (80 ml) hoisin sauce

2 tbsp (30 ml) rice wine vinegar

2 tbsp (30 ml) soy sauce

2 tbsp (30 ml) honey

1 tbsp (15 ml) fish sauce, optional

2 cloves garlic, grated

1 shallot, minced

1 tsp allspice

½ tsp cayenne pepper

Remove the membrane from the back of ribs—otherwise your ribs will be tough and chewy no matter how long you cook them. Flip the racks over so that the bones are facing up. Pry a finger (or a spoon) between the silvery membrane and the ribs to start pulling up the membrane—we like to do this between two of the rib bones. Once you have a piece of membrane pulled up, you should be able to easily pull the whole membrane off; use paper towels to grip this slippery membrane as needed. See the photos of this process on page 87.

Season the ribs all over with kosher salt and black pepper. Wrap the ribs and refrigerate for 4 hours, or overnight.

Heat the smoker to low—we're aiming for 225 to 275°F (110 to 135°C). Cook the ribs directly on the smoker for 3½ to 4 hours, or until the ribs are probe tender. While the ribs cook, make the BBQ Sauce, pickled vegetables and mayo for the sandwiches.

For the BBQ Sauce, combine the hoisin, rice wine vinegar, soy sauce, honey, fish sauce (if using), garlic, shallot, allspice and cayenne in a small bowl, and whisk to combine.

(continued)

For the Pickled Veggies

1 medium carrot, peeled and shaved into ribbons with a Y-shaped peeler

1 large English cucumber, thinly sliced

4 medium radishes, thinly sliced

1 medium red Fresno chile, thinly sliced

½ cup (120 ml) rice vinegar

2 tbsp (30 g) granulated sugar

1 tsp kosher salt

For the Mayo

½ cup (120 ml) mayo

¼ cup (60 ml) hoisin sauce

1 tbsp (15 ml) sriracha

2 tbsp (30 ml) lime juice

For the Sandwich

6–8 French rolls

1 cup (16 g) cilantro leaves

The pickled vegetables should marinate for at least 20 minutes, so toss together the carrot, cucumber, radishes and chile pepper with the rice vinegar, sugar and kosher salt in a large bowl while the ribs smoke.

Finally, whisk together the mayo, hoisin, sriracha and lime juice in another small bowl.

When the ribs have been smoking for about 4 hours, brush them with your BBQ Sauce. Cook for 10 minutes, paint with sauce and repeat three times total, about 30 more minutes of smoking. Remove the ribs from the smoker when they are super tender and the meat is pulling away from the bones.

When the ribs are cool enough to handle, remove the bones from the rib slabs. They should twist out easily leaving the meat intact. Cut the ribs into two bone sections.

Smear a bit of the mayo mixture on each French roll, then stack two rib bone sections on the bun, followed by about a ¼ cup (30 g) of the Pickled Veggies and fresh cilantro leaves. Serve immediately.

JUST THE TIP:
Swap out the French rolls with slider buns to make a tailgate friendly version.

BUFFALO CHICKEN PATTY *Sammie*

Serves: 4 | Prep Time: 30 minutes | Cook Time: 35 minutes

Thursdays were chicken patty day in the school cafeteria. They are nostalgic and delicious. How do we improve this? Make the patty from scratch. Then toss it with a spicy wing sauce and top it with homemade dressing. Do yourself a favor. Quadruple this recipe and freeze some uncooked patties. You'll want these on standby.

Caution Note: Frying on the grill is very dangerous. Make sure to read our safety notes on page 15 before proceeding. And again, please have a nice day.

For the Patties

1 lb (454 g) ground chicken (see Tip)

Kosher salt, for seasoning

Black pepper, for seasoning

1 tsp garlic powder

1 small yellow onion, grated

1 large egg

2 cups (112 g) panko breadcrumbs, divided

½ cup (120 ml) hot sauce

1 stick (8 tbsp; 113 g) salted butter

2 cloves garlic, grated

2 cups (480 ml) vegetable oil, for frying

Combine the chicken, a heavy pinch of kosher salt and black pepper, garlic powder, grated onion, egg and 1 cup (56 g) of the breadcrumbs in a large bowl. Use clean hands to gently combine the mixture and then divide into four patties, about 4 ounces (113 g) each. Set the patties on a baking sheet. Fill a plate with the remaining 1 cup (56 g) of breadcrumbs and press each patty into the breadcrumbs to coat well; don't forget to coat the rim of each patty, too. Set aside for about 20 minutes while you prep the sauces and the grill.

Combine the hot sauce, butter and garlic in a small saucepan (you'll cook this down a bit at the grill and then toss the chicken patties in it).

(continued)

BUFFALO CHICKEN PATTY *Sammie (continued)*

For the Blue Cheese Sauce

1 cup (240 ml) sour cream

¼ cup (60 ml) buttermilk

4 oz (113 g) blue cheese crumbles

1 bunch chives, finely chopped

¼ cup (15 g) chopped fresh parsley

Kosher salt, for seasoning

Black pepper, for seasoning

For the Sammies

4 potato buns

1 small head iceberg lettuce, cut into thin ribbons

1 beefsteak tomato, sliced

To make the Blue Cheese Sauce, in a small bowl, mix the sour cream, buttermilk, blue cheese, chives and parsley. Add a hefty pinch of kosher salt and black pepper. Chill this for about 15 minutes.

Heat the grill for medium-high direct heat. Fill a large high-sided pan with the vegetable oil. DO NOT OVERFILL the pan. Heat on the grill until the oil starts to shimmer; this will take about 5 minutes. You can cook the buffalo sauce on the grill at this time, too, if you've got room. Fry the patties in the hot oil for 4 minutes on each side, about 10 minutes total cook time, until they are delightfully golden, crispy and reach an internal temp of 160°F (70°C). Cool the chicken patties for 5 minutes before dunking in the buffalo sauce. Don't forget to toast your buns at the grill, too.

Build each sandwich on a potato bun, laying lettuce, chicken patty, blue cheese dressing and tomato, in that order. Get yourself some extra napkins before you dig in.

JUST THE TIP:

Ground dark meat is harder to find, but we love it for this sandwich. If you want the most flavorful chicken burger, ask your butcher to grind some chicken thighs for you.

Grill Marks

Are For Posers

Actually, We Have the Meats
ROAST BEEF SANDWICH

Serves: 6 to 8 | Prep Time: 20 minutes | Cook Time: 90 to 120 minutes

We're not above the occasional drive-thru roast beef sandwich. Every few years on a road trip we pass through to get one and within 1 minute remember why we like it so much better at home, grilled. Premium, fresh smoked beef with a creamy, spicy, homemade horseradish sauce wins.

Don't feel too bad, mister ten-gallon hat guy. You can have one of ours.

For the Horseradish Sauce

¼ cup (60 ml) mayo

¼ cup (60 ml) sour cream

1 tbsp (15 ml) buttermilk

2 tbsp (30 g) prepared horseradish

½ tsp garlic powder

¼ tsp Worcestershire sauce

Black pepper, for seasoning

For the Roast Beef

3 lb (1.4 kg) prime beef roast, such as ribeye

Kosher salt, for seasoning

Black pepper, for seasoning

1½ cups (360 ml) beef broth

6–8 pretzel rolls

Prepare the Horseradish Sauce by combining the mayo, sour cream, buttermilk, prepared horseradish, garlic powder and Worcestershire sauce in a large mixing bowl, and whisk to combine. Season with two cracks of black pepper. Chill in the fridge for at least 30 minutes or up to a day before using.

Season the beef roast liberally with kosher salt and black pepper, like a *ton* of salt and pepper. Set a roasting pan with a rack and place the beef on the rack. Pour the beef broth into the pan. Let it rest on the counter for an hour to come to room temp.

Heat the grill or oven to high heat, about 450°F (230°C). You can also make this in your oven and it will turn out just as delicious, but know that we *will* judge you for it.

Place the roast on the grill and after 10 minutes, lower the temp to 250°F (120°C). Continue to cook the roast until it hits an internal temp of 130°F (55°C; medium-rare), 80 to 90 minutes. Remove the roast and allow it to cool for 20 minutes.

Pour the beef drippings from the pan jus into a saucepan—run it through a fine-mesh strainer if you have one—and place on low heat.

Slice the beef as thin as you can. Pile it on the bottom bun and top it with the Horseradish Sauce.

Dip the top bun partially into the jus before putting it on top of the sandwich. For even more flavor, dip the beef in the jus before adding it to the sandwich or serve the sandwich with a side of jus for dipping.

Big Bro's PORK BELLY BLT

Serves: 4, makes 3 pounds (1.4 kg) pork belly | Prep Time: 36 hours | Cook Time: 90 minutes

Move over bacon, big bro is back in town. The rich, crispy pork belly achieves the perfect balance with maple and spicy chile. The pork belly requires a few steps and a little planning, but is super simple. And worth the wait. Ask your butcher for skin-off belly.

For the Pork Belly

¼ cup (58 g) kosher salt

¼ cup (34 g) black pepper

¼ cup (50 g) maple sugar

2 tbsp (28 g) brown sugar

1 tbsp (5 g) cayenne pepper

1 tbsp (7 g) sweet paprika

1 (3-lb [1.4-kg]) slab fresh pork belly

For the Sandwiches

8 slices soft white bread

½ cup (120 ml) mayo

1 head soft lettuce, such as Bibb

2 large heirloom tomatoes, sliced

Kosher salt, for seasoning

Black pepper, for seasoning

The pork belly will take 24 hours to cure before you smoke and chill it for cooking. Mix the kosher salt, black pepper, maple sugar, brown sugar, cayenne and sweet paprika in a bowl. Season the pork belly well on all sides with the cure, rubbing it in well. Tightly wrap the slab in plastic wrap and set it inside a rimmed baking sheet or 9 x 13–inch (23 x 33–cm) pan in the fridge. Turn the pork belly halfway through the 24-hour cure time.

Heat the smoker to low heat; we like apple or cherry wood here. Remove the pork belly from its wrap and rinse. Pat the pork belly dry with paper towels, and then set it directly on the smoker and cook for 2 hours or until the slab reaches 150°F (65°C).

Cool the pork belly for at least 30 minutes and then wrap tightly again in plastic wrap and sandwich it between two rimmed baking sheets. Weigh down the top baking sheet—a cast-iron skillet or bricks work well here. Chill the slab for at least 12 hours before using.

When you're ready to BLT, thinly slice the pork belly into ½-inch (1.3-cm) strips. Heat the grill to medium-high, set a skillet on the grill and add the pork belly pieces and, cook until crisp, about 8 minutes total. Remove the pork belly to a paper towel–lined plate. Toast the bread slices directly on the grill.

Build the BLTs by smearing 1 tablespoon (15 ml) of the mayo on each slice of bread. Put a piece of Bibb lettuce on the "bottom" piece of bread for each sandwich. Season the tomato slices with a pinch of kosher salt and black pepper, and divide among the sandwiches. Finally, add the pork belly and top with a second piece of bread. Slice the sandwiches on the diagonal—this is scientifically proven to make BLTs taste better—and serve immediately.

we told you a dozen times you can't make this claim

ITALIAN CHICKEN *Smashburger*

Serves: 8 | Prep Time: 30 minutes | Cook Time: 20 minutes

This chicken smashburger was reverse engineered from the ground up to be the perfect burger pairing with an Italian lager that is exactly .01 degrees above freezing. Sweet and spicy sauce, crispy chicken and melty, nutty cheese. Heaven. It turns out that chicken makes an excellent protein for smashburgers.

For the Chicken

2 lb (907 g) ground chicken

1 tbsp (2 g) Italian seasoning

2 tsp (3 g) garlic powder

½ tsp cayenne pepper

¼ cup (25 g) freshly grated Parmesan

¼ cup (15 g) chopped fresh parsley

Kosher salt, for seasoning

For the Spicy Tomato Sauce

2 tbsp (30 ml) olive oil

3 cloves garlic, chopped

1 (15-oz [425-g]) can crushed tomatoes

Kosher salt, for seasoning

2–3 Calabrian chiles, finely chopped

For the Sandwiches

8 buns, we like ciabatta buns but Kaiser rolls work well here too

8 slices Provolone cheese

8 leaves fresh basil

Combine the ground chicken, Italian seasoning, garlic powder, cayenne, Parmesan and parsley in a bowl. Add a hefty sprinkle of kosher salt and then use clean hands to gently work the mixture together. Divide the mixture into eight rounds—not patties, but loose rounds to smash later.

To make the Spicy Tomato Sauce, heat the olive oil in a large skillet over medium-high heat. Add the garlic to the oil and cook just until fragrant, about 1 minute. Add the crushed tomatoes and a big pinch of kosher salt. Finish the sauce with the chiles and remove from the heat.

Heat the grill for two-zone cooking. Toast the burger buns over high heat and then move to indirect heat to keep warm.

Heat a large skillet over direct heat. Working in batches of two, add two of the rounds to the skillet at a time. Use a large flat spatula to press down hard on each patty for 2 minutes. Flip and continue cooking—the goal is a crisp, craggled, super-thin patty. Move the first two patties to indirect heat and top each with a slice of Provolone. Repeat with the remaining chicken rounds. While you're still at the grill, top the chicken patties with a scoop of the sauce.

Build the sandwiches by placing one patty on each bun and topping with fresh basil.

GOOD MORNING
BREAKFAST
2nd Breakfast and Brunch

For some reason the grill is rarely thought of as the heat source of choice for breakfast. We're trying to change that. Every Sunday should start with lighting a grill and drinking some coffee with a little crisp in the air. The food also benefits from smoke and fire. Baked eggs, smoky sausage, wood-fired bacon and on and on.

Remember, with a few cast-iron or carbon steel pans and a griddle, you can do 100% of your morning feast on the grill. In fact, our Food Network television career started when we cooked our Arthur's Stuffed French Toast (page 157) for Guy Fieri directly on the grates of the grill. We were crowned "best bite of the night."

Bacon? Indirect in a sheet tray. Pancakes? Cook 'em in a cast-iron griddle pan on the grill. Scrambled eggs? Carbon steel pan. Biscuits? Wood fired in the pellet grill. Blueberry muffins? Indirect in the gas grill. Hell, we even keep a special ten foot (3 m) long high amp extension cord outside for when we make waffles for a crowd while using our gas grill on low to keep them warm.

Pro Tip: Breakfast is the best meal of the day to cook in the hottest part of the summer. Get your grill reps in before the sun is scorching.

Arthur's STUFFED FRENCH TOAST

Serves: 8 | Prep Time: 30 minutes | Cook Time: 40 minutes

Mark's son Arthur loves this creamy, custardy, lemony French toast with all the amazing flavor benefits of cooking on the grill. Is there anything else we need to say? You set yourself up for an easy breezy morning by prepping everything the night before. Make the egg custard, strawberry syrup sauce and ricotta filling. Heck, you can even stuff 'em. Just don't dip 'em until they're about to hit the grill.

For the Strawberry Sauce-Up

2 lb (908 g) fresh strawberries, washed, stemmed and halved (see Tip)

1 large lemon, washed and dried

1/3 cup (80 ml) maple syrup

Kosher salt, for seasoning

For the Lemon Ricotta Filling

2 cups (492 g) whole milk ricotta

3/4 cup (180 ml) lemon curd

1/4 tsp kosher salt

For the French Toast

6 large eggs

4 large egg yolks

1 cup (240 ml) heavy cream

1 tsp vanilla extract

2 tsp (3 g) ground cinnamon

1/2 tsp kosher salt

16 slices Texas toast—style sliced bread, about 1 loaf

1/4 cup (60 ml) vegetable oil

Powdered sugar, for serving

Fresh mint leaves, for serving

Heat the grill for indirect cooking. Set a medium saucepan over direct heat and add the strawberries, the zest and juice of the lemon, maple syrup and a pinch of kosher salt. Bring the mixture to a simmer and cook until the berries are impossibly soft and the mixture has reduced a bit, about 10 minutes.

Make the Lemon Ricotta Filling by whisking together the ricotta with the lemon curd and kosher salt.

For the French toast, in a large mixing bowl, whisk together the eggs, egg yolks, heavy cream, vanilla extract, cinnamon and salt. Set a cooling rack inside a rimmed baking sheet. Dollop 1/3 cup (80 ml) of the Lemon Ricotta Filling on a slice of bread and top it with another slice of bread, then dip in the custard mixture. Set the French toasts on the cooling rack to absorb the batter while you dunk the other pieces and get the grill set.

Make sure you carefully oil the grill grates generously with vegetable oil before setting the stuffed French toast over direct heat (see page 21). Cook four pieces at a time, flipping after 3 minutes. Once the French toasts have a nice char (and OK, maybe a few grill marks) move them to the indirect side of the grill to make sure the custard is cooked through, about 10 minutes. Repeat with the other four stuffed French toasts.

Serve the French toast with a dusting of powdered sugar, a drizzle of the Strawberry Sauce-Up and a few fresh mint leaves.

JUST THE TIP:

You can absolutely swap the fresh berries here for frozen. No need to thaw, just give the sauce-up a little more time to cook and use your spatula to break up the berries once they've softened.

Fey's Favorite BREAKFAST BURRITO

Serves: 4 to 6 | Prep Time: 15 minutes | Cook Time: 20 minutes

This is a neatly wrapped-up cowboy breakfast all-in-one topped with a smoky, peppery, rich and spicy chipotle cream sauce. We buy our burrito tortillas at a restaurant supply store so we can get the jumbo ones they use at our favorite Mexican food trucks. If you're cooking for a crowd, you can get started early, then wrap each burrito in foil and put it in the oven on warm so you can serve them all at once.

For the Burrito

1 lb (454 g) breakfast sausage

8 oz (226 g) bacon, chopped

2 tbsp (30 ml) olive oil, plus more if needed

2 cups (170 g) shredded hash brown potatoes, from the freezer or fresh (see Tip)

8 large eggs

½ tsp kosher salt

4–6 big-ass tortillas, at least 10 inches (25 cm)

1 cup (113 g) shredded Cheddar cheese

For the Chipotle Cream Sauce

½ cup (120 ml) mayo

½ cup (120 ml) Mexican crema

1 tbsp (15 ml) lime juice

3 chipotles in adobo

1 tbsp (15 ml) of the adobo sauce

¼ cup (4 g) chopped fresh cilantro, plus more for serving

Kosher salt, for seasoning

Heat the grill for medium-high direct heat. Heat two large cast-iron skillets directly on the grill. In one, crumble the sausage into the pan and add the bacon. Cook, stirring often, until the bacon is crisped and the sausage is cooked through, about 8 minutes. In the other, heat the olive oil and add the hash browns in a single layer. Cook, without stirring, for 6 minutes, then use a thin spatula to flip and cook for 2 minutes more. Move the meat skillet off the heat and set aside. Remove the hash browns to a plate.

Meanwhile, crack the eggs into a bowl, season with kosher salt and whisk to combine. If needed, add a tablespoon (15 ml) of oil to the pan—there may still be plenty from the hash browns—then add the egg mixture. Cook the scrambled eggs by gently turning the curds as they cook. Do your best not to overcook the eggs; some still wet-looking areas are OK—these babies are going back on the grill in a bit.

Build the burritos: Lay out a tortilla and layer on the sausage mixture followed by a sprinkle of cheese, then hash browns and then eggs. Fold the sides of the burrito in and then roll up the burrito. Set aside while you make the chipotle sauce.

To make the Chipotle Cream Sauce, combine the mayo, crema, lime juice, chipotles and their sauce and the cilantro in a food processor. Season with a pinch of kosher salt and process until smooth.

For serving, crisp the burritos over medium-high direct heat, for just 2 minutes per side. Serve with a drizzle of the Chipotle Cream Sauce and a sprinkle of fresh cilantro.

JUST THE TIP:

You can find ready-to-cook hash brown potatoes in the frozen aisle, or grab the "fresh" version near the eggs in most grocery stores.

Red Flannel HIPSTER HASH

Serves: 6 | Prep Time: 25 minutes | Cook Time: 30 minutes

Hash might be the perfect all-in-one breakfast meal. The star of this dish is the beets, which are roasted, transforming them from bitter and earthy to rich and sweet. Add some mild potatoes, nutty squash and salty corned beef, then crisp it up. Oh, and we've included the perfect sauce for hash. The runny yolk of a fried egg. This hash sure is hard to beet. (Get it? You know "beet" instead of "beat"? OK, forget it.)

1 lb (454 g) medium-sized beets, about 4

1 lb (454 g) small red potatoes

1 small butternut squash, about 1 lb (454 g), halved and seeds removed

4 tbsp (56 g) salted butter

1 large onion, chopped

2 tsp (10 g) kosher salt, plus more for seasoning the eggs

8 oz (226 g) cooked corned beef, diced

1 tsp Worcestershire sauce

¼ cup (15 g) chopped fresh parsley, plus more for serving

2 tbsp (30 ml) olive oil

6 large eggs

Heat the grill for two-zone cooking. Wrap the beets in an aluminum foil pouch. Place the potatoes and squash directly on the grill grates over indirect heat. Roast the beets, potatoes and squash until mostly tender, about 30 minutes. Remove from the grill and cool. Peel the beets, and chop the beets and potatoes into 1-inch (2.5-cm) pieces. Scoop the flesh out of the squash with a big-ass spoon and roughly chop.

Set a large cast-iron skillet over direct heat. Melt the butter and add the onion, and cook until tender and beginning to brown, about 8 minutes. Add the beets, squash and potatoes, and season with kosher salt, then shake the pan to distribute everything into an even layer. Sprinkle the corned beef over the vegetables. Cook without stirring until the potatoes and beets are golden, about 10 minutes. Season with the Worcestershire sauce and parsley.

Meanwhile, heat the olive oil in a carbon steel skillet over medium heat until shimmering. Crack the eggs into a large bowl and carefully add to the pan—this might seem fussy but it ensures all the eggs cook at the same rate and no shells end up in your hash. Season with a pinch of kosher salt and cook the eggs for 3 to 4 minutes, or until the white is set and the edges are just beginning to brown. Remove from the pan. Serve the hash topped with a fried egg.

Basque Chorizo and
POTATO FRITTATA, BAI!

Serves: 10 to 12 | Prep Time: 25 minutes | Cook Time: 20 minutes

There may be no better breakfast duo than chorizo and potato. It's the Hall and Oates of breakfast. The Starsky and Hutch of brunch. This can be a simple rustic breakfast, the centerpiece of a bougie brunch or a Sunday meal prep dish for a busy workweek.

For the Frittata

8 oz (226 g) Basque-style chorizo (see Tip)

3 tbsp (45 ml) olive oil

1 lb (454 g) Yukon gold potatoes, about 2 medium potatoes, quartered and sliced in ¼-inch (6-mm) pieces

1 large red bell pepper, sliced

1 medium yellow onion, thinly sliced

4 cloves garlic, minced

Kosher salt, for seasoning

8 large eggs

⅓ cup (80 ml) heavy cream

¼ cup (25 g) finely grated Parmesan

½ tsp freshly ground black pepper

For the Salad

¼ cup (60 ml) olive oil

¼ cup (60 ml) sherry vinegar

½ tsp Dijon mustard

½ tsp kosher salt

5 oz (142 g) arugula

¼ cup (15 g) finely chopped fresh parsley

2 oz (57 g) Manchego cheese, shaved

Prep your grill for two-zone cooking or heat the oven to 400°F (205°C). Grill the chorizo over high heat for 2 minutes on each side. Remove to cool, and then quarter and slice into ¼-inch (6-cm) pieces.

Heat the olive oil in a 10-inch (25-cm) cast-iron skillet over medium-high heat. Add the chorizo followed by the potatoes, bell pepper, onion, garlic and a big pinch of kosher salt to the pan, and toss to coat them in the oil. Cook the vegetable mixture for 8 to 10 minutes, stirring regularly, until the potatoes are tender. While the potatoes cook, make the egg mixture.

Whisk the eggs, heavy cream, Parmesan, a pinch of kosher salt and black pepper in a medium-sized mixing bowl until smooth. When the potatoes are tender, add the egg mixture to the hot pan, move to the lower heat side of the grill or the oven and cook for 18 to 22 minutes. The frittata is finished when the center is set and the top is just beginning to brown.

While the frittata cooks, make the salad. In a medium mixing bowl, whisk together the oil, vinegar, mustard and kosher salt. Add the arugula and parsley, and toss them to coat. Add the Manchego and toss once more to combine.

Slide the frittata out onto a serving place, slice in wedges and serve with the salad.

JUST THE TIP:

If you can't find Basque chorizo, Andouille is a readily available substitute. Allow the sausage to cool down before you slice it so all the juices stay in the sausage! Make sure you don't use Spanish or Mexican chorizo. They are wildly different.

Apple Pie PANCAKE

Serves: 6 to 8 | Prep Time: 20 minutes | Cook Time: 35 minutes

For us, a giant pancake that serves 6 to 8 people is already enough of a reason to get out of bed in the morning. But when you add caramelized apples and cinnamon sugar, it becomes the thing your family looks forward to all week. Bonus: If there are leftovers (which there won't be) this makes a great coffee sidecar on your way to work.

1 cup (125 g) all-purpose flour

1 tbsp (15 g) granulated sugar

1 tsp baking powder

½ tsp kosher salt

2 large eggs

1 cup (240 ml) buttermilk

2 large apples, peeled, cored and sliced

2 tbsp (28 g) salted butter

3 tbsp (42 g) light brown sugar

Cinnamon-sugar, for serving (see Tip)

Maple syrup, for serving

Whisk together the flour, granulated sugar, baking powder and kosher salt in a large bowl. Add the eggs and buttermilk, and whisk to combine—don't worry about some lumps and don't overmix the batter. Set aside to rest while you cook the apples.

Heat the grill for medium direct heat. Heat a 10-inch (25-cm) skillet directly on the grill grates. Add the apples and butter, and cook until the apples are softened, about 10 minutes. Sprinkle on the brown sugar and cook for an additional 2 to 3 minutes until the sugar is caramel-like.

Press the apples down a bit with a spatula. Pour the prepared batter into the apples. Close the grill and cook for 18 to 20 minutes. Remove the skillet from the grill and cool for about 10 minutes.

To serve, invert a serving plate onto the skillet and carefully (using heatproof gloves) turn over the plate and skillet together. Top the pancake with cinnamon-sugar and cut into wedges to serve. Eat with maple syrup and more cinnamon-sugar, because why not?

JUST THE TIP:

We don't want to assume that you have cinnamon-sugar just hanging out in your pantry (do you not love late night cinnamon toast?!), so here's how we mix it. Shake up ¼ cup (60 g) of granulated sugar with 2 tablespoons (16 g) of ground cinnamon and a pinch of kosher salt.

CAST-IRON BISCUITS *with Diablo Gravy*

Serves: 6 to 8 | Prep Time: 45 minutes | Cook Time: 90 minutes

Southern biscuits and gravy just got its 23andMe results back and it turns out there's a first cousin in Italy the family never knew about. They're flaky and smokin' hot. This dish is buttery, rich, spicy and aromatic. If you're really feeling crazy, top this off with a few fried eggs. Or don't. See if we care.

For the Biscuits

1 cup (2 sticks) plus 2 tbsp (482 g) unsalted butter, cold from the fridge

1 tbsp (14 g) unsalted butter, softened

4 cups (500 g) all-purpose flour, plus extra for dusting

1 tbsp (14 g) baking powder

1 tsp kosher salt

1 tsp baking soda

2¼ cups (540 ml) buttermilk, cold from the fridge

For the Diablo Gravy

2 tbsp (30 ml) olive oil

16 oz (454 g) hot Italian bulk sausage

1 tsp finely chopped fresh oregano leaves

2 cloves garlic, minced

¼ cup (31 g) all-purpose flour

3 cups (720 ml) whole milk

2–3 Calabrian chiles, finely chopped

Kosher salt, for seasoning

Crushed red pepper, for serving (optional)

¼ cup (6 g) fresh basil leaves, rolled and sliced into ribbons, for topping

Heat the grill or smoker for medium-high heat between 400 and 425°F (205 and 220°C). Quickly grate the cold butter on the large side of a box grater onto a parchment paper–lined plate. Stick this plate of grated butter in the fridge for 30 minutes while you prep the rest of the ingredients. Grease a 12-inch (30-cm) cast-iron skillet with the softened butter and set aside.

In a large bowl, whisk together the flour, baking powder, kosher salt and baking soda. Add the grated chilled butter to the dry ingredients. Use your fingertips to press the butter into the flour, breaking it into smaller pieces and leaving some shreds larger, and finally making a well in the center of this mixture. Add the cold buttermilk and stir swiftly with a spatula to mix everything into a shaggy batter. It should all come together before being dumped out onto a flour-covered work surface.

Gently pat the biscuit dough out into an even rectangle and sprinkle with additional flour. Fold the dough onto itself in thirds—fold one side over the middle and the other side over that fold, like an envelope. Dust the dough with flour and roll out into another even rectangle. Repeat folding and rolling two more times, for a total of four folds, until the dough is somewhat smooth and springy. Roll the dough out to ½-inch (1.3-cm) thickness and use a large biscuit cutter to punch the dough out into 3-inch (8-cm) rounds. Place the biscuits in the prepared skillet so that they all touch. Refold and cut more biscuits out from the remaining dough.

Bake the biscuits, covered, on the grill, for 12 to 15 minutes, until risen and golden brown. Remove the biscuits from the grill and lower it to medium heat.

To make the Diablo Gravy, in another large skillet or ovenproof pan, heat the olive oil until it shimmers. Add the sausage, breaking it into small pieces. Brown the sausage until it is no longer pink, about 8 minutes. Add the oregano and garlic, and cook until fragrant. Sprinkle the sausage with the flour, turn to coat it and cook until the flour smells like pancakes, about 1 minute.

Remove the pan from the heat, then quickly add the milk and stir to prevent lumps from forming. Return the pan to the grill and cook until the gravy thickens, 4 to 5 minutes. Turn off the heat, add the chiles and kosher salt. Taste and season with additional kosher salt and crushed red pepper (if using). Serve the gravy over split biscuits and top with basil chiffonade.

BELGIAN WAFFLE *Breakfast Sliders*

Serves: 8 to 10 | Prep Time: 60 minutes | Cook Time: 45 minutes

We already know this is going to be your favorite breakfast sandwich. You just need to make it once. There are a few ways to make the waffles. We often run an extension cord, cook them outside and keep them warm on the grill. Or if super rugged, grab a cast-iron griddle and cook them right over the coals. Show off. You won't want store-bought sausage ever again, by the way.

For the Waffles

2 cups (250 g) all-purpose flour

½ cup (100 g) granulated sugar

1 tbsp (14 g) baking powder

Kosher salt

2 large eggs

1 cup (240 ml) whole milk

8 oz (227 g; 2 sticks) salted butter, melted

For the Spicy Maple Butter

4 oz (113 g; 1 stick) salted butter, at room temperature

¼ cup (60 ml) maple syrup

1 tsp ground cinnamon

½ tsp cayenne pepper

Make the waffle batter and the Spicy Maple Butter in advance. For the waffles, whisk together the flour, sugar, baking powder and a pinch of kosher salt in a large bowl. Add the eggs, milk and butter, and whisk to combine—don't worry about some lumps and don't overmix the batter. Set aside to rest.

For the Spicy Maple Butter, mash the butter, maple syrup, cinnamon and cayenne in a small bowl. Chill while you prep the sausage.

For the Homemade Sausage

1 lb (454 g) ground pork

2 tbsp (30 ml) olive oil

2 cloves garlic, grated

1 tbsp (2 g) dried sage

1 tsp brown sugar

1 tsp coriander

1 tsp fennel seeds

½ tsp red pepper flakes

Kosher salt, for seasoning

Black pepper, for seasoning

For the Fluffy Eggs

8 large eggs

¼ cup (60 ml) heavy cream

Kosher salt, for seasoning

2 tbsp (28 g) salted butter

8 oz (226 g) shredded sharp Cheddar

Start the sausage by dumping the pork, olive oil, garlic, sage, sugar, coriander, fennel and red pepper flakes into a large bowl. Add a three-finger pinch of kosher salt and plenty of black pepper. Use a wooden spoon to beat the mixture together to emulsify, you want this stuff sticky and homogenous—this will be the difference between this feeling like sausage and not a pork patty. Divide the pork into ¼-cup (50-g) portions and flatten into disks.

For the eggs, whisk together the eggs, heavy cream and a pinch of kosher salt in a medium bowl.

Bring everything out to the grill and set it for two-zone cooking. Heat the waffle griddle over high heat and cook the waffle batter first. Each waffle will use about ½ cup (120 ml) of batter, depending on your iron. Move the finished waffles to a cooling rack set over the indirect side of the grill, and keep them warm while you cook the sausage and eggs.

Cook the sausage in a large cast-iron skillet over direct heat. You don't need any additional fat, just cook the sausage patties until browned before flipping and browning on the second side, about 8 minutes total cook time. Remove the sausage from the pan to the indirect side of the grill to keep warm.

Finally, cook the eggs; we're going for a kind of fluffy, omelet-like egg here. Melt the butter in the cast-iron skillet and add the eggs. Cook without stirring for 2 minutes, then add the cheese and fold the sides of the egg up onto itself—you're making a little pocket of cheese with the eggs. Then flip the whole square of eggs over to finish cooking.

Remove the eggs from the skillet and cut into eight squares. Serve the waffles with a smear of Spicy Maple Butter, a sausage patty and a square of eggs.

THINGS
YOU EAT
While Grilling

We've thought long and hard about this section, and to be honest, it's one of the most exciting parts of this cookbook. Why? Because this is the stuff that you eat while you are cooking stuff to eat. From dips and grilled potstickers (page 177) to Pizza Bombs (page 184) and chicken pot pie potato skins (page 187)—take your pick of these awesome recipes and make sure you make them before you crank up the grill.

Come On In, the Water's Fine
SMOKED TROUT DIP

Serves: 6 to 8 | Prep Time: 48 hours | Cook Time: 2 hours

This make-ahead dip will yield zero leftovers. The star of this dish, the steelhead trout, is the ocean-bound cousin of the freshwater rainbow trout and frequent salmon doppelganger. It has the same pink flesh as salmon and all the same nutrients but is less fatty. It takes the smoke well and then flakes perfectly into the dip. All that being said, you can use rainbow trout for this dish if you can't find steelhead.

For the Smoked Trout

2 skin-on steelhead or rainbow trout fillets

½ cup (115 g) kosher salt

½ cup (110 g) light brown sugar

1 tbsp (6 g) lemon zest

3 scallions, roughly chopped

For the Dip

½ cup (112 g) mascarpone cheese

½ cup (120 ml) crème fraîche

1 large lemon, washed and dried

1 small red onion, finely chopped

3 tbsp (25 g) capers

¼ cup (15 g) fresh parsley, finely chopped

Kosher salt, for seasoning

Black pepper, for seasoning

For Serving

Water crackers

Fresh vegetables, such as endive, celery or petite peppers

Before smoking, the trout needs at least 2 days to cure and then dry. Start by deboning the trout pieces; your fishmonger will have done most of this work but just to be sure, run your fingers over the flesh and use a pair of pliers to pull out the obvious bones.

Combine the kosher salt, sugar, lemon zest and scallions in a food processor, and pulse ten to twelve times to combine. Pack this brine onto the trout, then smoosh the trout together with the flesh sides facing in and then tightly cover the fish in plastic wrap. Stash the wrapped fish in the fridge for 24 to 36 hours in a rimmed baking dish. Turn every 12 hours.

After 24 to 36 hours, remove the trout from the fridge, take off the plastic wrap and rinse off the brine. Then set the fillets out, flesh-side up, on a cooling rack set inside a rimmed baking sheet and return to the fridge for 12 hours.

Heat the smoker to low with alder wood. Set the cooling rack directly on the smoker and smoke the trout until it reaches 145°F (65°C), usually about 2 hours. Keep the smoker temp as close to 200°F (95°C) as possible—you can add a baking pan of ice to keep things cool.

After smoking, cool the trout for at least 1 hour before making the dip, or cool completely and store for up to 3 days.

Flake or chop the trout (discarding the skin) and add to a large mixing bowl. Dump in the mascarpone, crème fraîche, the zest and juice of 1 lemon, red onion, capers and parsley. Fold everything together, taste and add kosher salt and black pepper to taste. Serve the dip with water crackers and fresh vegetables for dipping.

MARK'S BBQ OYSTERS
with *West Carolina Mignonette*

There isn't a West Carolina

Serves: 2 to 4 | Prep Time: 30 minutes | Cook Time: 15 minutes

Combining freshy, briny oysters with the taste of the grill and zippy mignonette BBQ sauce results in the perfect bite. Salty, slightly smoky, acidic, spicy and sweet. We always get our oysters from the coldest water possible. This ensures mild, sweet and tender oysters. If you can't find rock salt, white rice can be subbed for holding the oysters.

For the Oysters

12–16 medium to large oysters

3 cups (690 g) coarse salt

For the West Carolina Mignonette

1 cup (240 ml) apple cider vinegar

½ cup (120 ml) ketchup

1 tbsp (15 ml) Dijon mustard

1 small shallot, minced

1 tsp prepared horseradish

½ tsp red pepper flakes

Scrub the oysters clean. Shuck the oysters: Working with one at a time, nestle the oyster with the cup side down in a clean kitchen towel. Place the heel of your non-dominant hand on the oyster and then gently force the tip of an oyster knife into the oyster's hinge. Once you've got the oyster knife firmly in the hinge, rotate the oyster knife, twisting it up and down until the hinge releases. When it does, wipe off the tip of your knife on the towel, and then work your knife under the top shell and sever the muscle that connects the shells. Discard the top shell and check the oyster for any shell fragments, but also give each one a whiff (trash any that are stinky, though this is relatively rare; good oysters should smell briny, not fishy). Use the oyster knife to also loosen the oyster from the bottom shell—this will make eating even easier later. Fill a cast-iron skillet with the coarse salt and nestle the oysters in the salt.

Make the mignonette by whisking together the apple cider vinegar, ketchup, mustard, shallot, horseradish and red pepper flakes in a medium-sized bowl. Set aside. This sauce keeps well in the fridge for weeks and tastes as great splashed on leftover fries as it does fresh fish.

Heat the grill for high direct heat. Set the whole skillet of oyster on the grill, cover the grill and cook until the oysters plump and begin to curl, 2 to 3 minutes. Spoon the West Carolina Mignonette onto the oysters and serve immediately.

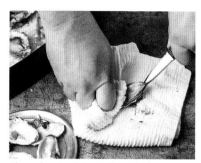

Place the tip of the knife in the hinge

Twist the knife to pop the hinge

Loosen the top shell

Remove the top shell

GRILLED STICKERS *with Szechuan Chile Sauce*

Serves: 6 to 8, makes about 40 potstickers | Prep Time: 12 hours | Cook Time: 15 minutes

You know what makes this recipe great? Everything. Cooking these stickers on the grill gives them some smoky and earthy fire-kissed flavor to go with our "sneaker-heat" Szechuan Chile Sauce.

For the Szechuan Chile Sauce

1 tsp Szechuan peppercorns

⅓ cup (80 ml) soy sauce

3 tbsp (45 ml) honey

1 tbsp (15 ml) mirin

1 tsp sesame oil

3 cloves garlic, grated

2 tbsp (12 g) grated fresh ginger

1 tbsp (15 ml) garlic chile paste

For the Potstickers

1 lb (454 g) ground pork

2 heads baby bok choy, finely chopped

4 cloves garlic, grated

2 tbsp (12 g) grated fresh ginger

2 tbsp (30 ml) soy sauce

1 tbsp (15 ml) mirin

⅓ cup (80 ml) water, plus more for sealing the potstickers

1 (10- to 12-oz [283- to 340-g]) package round Asian dumpling wrappers (about 3½ inches [9 cm] in diameter, sometimes labeled gyoza or potsticker wrappers)

Vegetable oil, for greasing

Heat a small skillet over medium heat and toast the peppercorns until fragrant, 1 to 2 minutes. Remove from the heat and crush the peppercorns; you can use a mortar and pestle or just beat them with a meat mallet. Combine the peppercorns with the soy sauce, honey, mirin, sesame oil, garlic, ginger and chile paste in a small bowl. Whisk together and let meld overnight.

Mix up the potsticker filling in a large bowl. Combine the ground pork, baby bok choy, garlic, ginger, soy sauce, mirin and water, and stir vigorously until the mixture is sticky.

Fill a small bowl with water for sealing the potstickers. Lay six wrappers on a clean work surface and drop 1 tablespoon (15 g) of filling just off the center of each wrapper, leaving about a ½-inch (1.3-cm) border. Dip your finger in the water and trace around the edge of a wrapper to moisten. Fold the wrapper in half, bringing the bottom up to the top, pressing to seal around the filling. You can pleat the potstickers, if desired. Move the filled potstickers to a rimmed baking sheet, setting them on their spine to create a flat bottom. Repeat with the remaining filling and wrappers.

Heat the grill to medium heat. Carefully grease the grill grates generously with vegetable oil and add the potstickers directly to the grill. Cook the potstickers for 5 minutes, or until the wrappers have cooked enough to release from the grate, then turn the potstickers and cook for 3 to 4 minutes more. Move to a serving platter and serve with the Szechuan Chile Sauce.

JUST THE TIP:

Drizzle some oil on a clean kitchen towel and wipe down the grates to make sure the stickers don't stick. Use this method whenever you need to oil your grates.

Bougie STICKS

Serves: 4 to 6 | Prep Time: 10 minutes | Cook Time: 15 minutes

No matter where we are in the world, when we go out to eat, one of the things we almost always look for is a place that has mozzarella sticks on the menu. In fact, before Mark named his son Arthur, he was pretty close to naming him Mozz. True story. Well, with this twist on a familiar favorite, we lose the mozz cheese and replace it with cheese's gift from the grilling gods: halloumi. This nutty and salty cheese can stand up to the grates and the fire of a grill—so go wild and up your humble cheese stick game. Get Bougie.

1 lb (454 g) halloumi cheese

2 tbsp (30 ml) olive oil

2 oz (57 g) finely grated Parmesan cheese

1 cup (240 ml) Sheet-Pan Red Sauce (page 83) or your favorite marinara

Heat the grill for high, direct heat cooking. Cut the halloumi into ½-inch (1.3-cm) sticks. Brush the halloumi with the olive oil and season with Parmesan cheese—you may have to press it on to get it to adhere. Grill the halloumi directly on the grill grates to brown, turning every 2 minutes, for a total of 6 to 8 minutes. Remove the cheese to a serving platter and serve with the Sheet-Pan Red Sauce for dipping.

QUESO *Super Fundido*

Serves: 6 to 8 | Prep Time: 10 minutes | Cook Time: 15 minutes

We aren't really sure if there is anything better on the planet than a dish full of molten lava cheese with spicy chorizo in it. Give this recipe a whirl and we dare you to dispute us. But just make sure you have enough chips because once you start . . .

8 oz (226 g) Mexican chorizo

2 cups (226 g) shredded Oaxaca cheese

2 cups (226 g) shredded Monterey Jack

Pico de Gallo (page 30), for serving

Tortilla chips, for serving

Heat the grill to medium-high heat. Add a large cast-iron pan. Allow it to heat up, then add the chorizo. Cook, breaking up the chorizo into small pieces, 6 to 7 minutes. Remove the chorizo to a paper towel–lined plate.

Divide the cooked chorizo between 6 to 8 mini cast-iron skillets (or one 8-inch [20-cm] one if you don't love cheesy fun). Top each skillet with some of the Oaxaca and Monterey Jack cheeses. Place the mini skillets on the grill and cook long enough to melt the cheese, about 8 minutes.

Remove the skillets from the grill, then top with a spoonful of Pico de Gallo and serve with chips for dipping.

Whip It Good SMOKED FETA DIP

Serves: 6 to 8 | Prep Time: 15 minutes | Cook Time: 10 minutes

You're gonna wanna whip it good for sure with this super simple crowd-pleaser. And what's better than grilled and garlicky feta cheese that's lapped up with our Quick Grilled Flatbread (page 102) or some fresh snappy veggies? Nothing. And if you want to add a little heat to this dish for a twist, start by throwing in some chopped hot peppers or even your favorite hot sauce.

1 (8-oz [226-g]) block feta cheese

4 tbsp (60 ml) olive oil, divided

Kosher salt, for seasoning

½ cup (120 ml) whole milk Greek yogurt

½ cup (120 ml) mayo

2 cloves garlic, grated

1 large lemon, washed and dried

Pita bread or Quick Grilled Flatbread (page 102)

Sliced vegetables, for dipping

Heat the grill for medium-high indirect cooking. Brush the block of feta with 2 tablespoons (30 ml) of the olive oil and season well with kosher salt. Put the block of feta directly on the grill grates over direct heat and cook until lightly browned, about 2 minutes. Remove the feta—a fish spatula is best for this.

Crumble the grilled feta, reserving a few tablespoons for garnishing, and add to a food processor along with the yogurt, mayo, garlic, zest and juice of the lemon, and a heavy pinch of kosher salt. Blend until smooth and doubled in volume, about 5 minutes total.

Move the feta dip to a serving bowl and drizzle with the remaining 2 tablespoons (30 ml) of olive oil and the reserved feta. Serve with pita bread or Quick Grilled Flatbread and vegetables for dipping.

Zoe's SPANISH TOAST

Serves: 6 | Prep Time: 15 minutes | Cook Time: 10 minutes

This is Fey's kid Zoe's absolute favorite thing to eat for breakfast, lunch, dinner and everything in between. It's the super simple, salty, fruity and earthy flavors that meld together so well with the richness of the ham and the charcoal-laden grilled baguette. Fey has had this many times in Spain, and now Zoe wants to move there just so she can have authentic Spanish toast all the time (in the meantime, she really likes this recipe).

2 large ripe Roma tomatoes

1 clove garlic, grated

½ cup (120 ml) olive oil, divided

Kosher salt, for seasoning

1 baguette

4 oz (113 g) thinly sliced Manchego cheese

4 oz (113 g) thinly sliced jamon or prosciutto

Halve the tomatoes and scoop out the seeds and pulp. Grate the tomato halves on the large holes of a box grater into a mixing bowl. Add the grated garlic, ¼ cup (60 ml) of olive oil and a pinch of kosher salt.

Heat the grill to medium-high heat. Cut the baguette on a bias into about twenty ½-inch (1.3-cm) pieces. Brush the bread with the remaining ¼ cup (60 ml) of olive oil (you may not need to use all of it) and sprinkle it with kosher salt. Grill the baguette directly on the grates for 1 to 2 minutes per side, or until they are crisp and golden brown. Remove the bread to a serving tray and gently press down with a thumb into the center of each piece to create a little bread boat (aw, how cute).

Spoon the tomato mixture onto each baguette piece. Top each little boat with cheese and cured meat, and rejoice in being an after-school-snack hero.

JUST THE TIP:

Lose the jamon for a killer vegetarian appetizer.

PIZZA *Bombs*

Serves: 4 to 6 | Prep Time: 20 minutes | Cook Time: 20 minutes

Pizza. Bombs. Need we say more? We didn't think so. Make a batch all for yourself on game day or make a truckload for the neighborhood; either way you'll be the happiest person on the block.

2 tbsp (60 ml) olive oil, plus more for greasing

1 (15-oz [425-g]) can crushed tomatoes

3 cloves garlic, minced

Kosher salt, for seasoning

1 lb (454 g) pizza dough

4 oz (113 g) pancetta

4 oz (113 g) pepperoni slices

8 oz (226 g) shredded part-skim mozzarella

4 oz (113 g) grated Parmesan cheese

Heat the grill to medium heat. Brush a standard muffin pan with olive oil. Combine the tomatoes, garlic, olive oil and a pinch of kosher salt in a small bowl.

Roll the pizza dough out to a 10 x 16–inch (25 x 41–cm) rectangle. Spread the sauce evenly over the dough. Add the pancetta and pepperoni, and sprinkle on the mozzarella and Parmesan. Starting with the long end closest to you, roll the dough up onto itself to create a spiral. Pinch the dough to seal. Cut the tube into twelve rolls about ½ inch (1.3 cm) thick. Put one roll into each well of the muffin pan.

Bake the pizza bombs on the grill with the lid closed for 18 to 20 minutes. Remove from the pan immediately and serve warm.

Chicken Pot Pie POTATO SKINS—YEP

Serves: 4 to 6 | Prep Time: 60 minutes | Cook Time: 90 minutes

We decided that we wanted to create a recipe mashup of two of our very favorite things: chicken pot pie and potato skins. Seems logical, right? Hell yeah, it is. So, close your eyes and imagine a buttery, flavorful and steamy chicken pot pie layered into a perfectly baked russet potato skin topped with puff pastry. Now, open your eyes and make this dish. You're welcome.

6 small russet potatoes

3 tbsp (42 g) salted butter

1 small onion, diced

Kosher salt, for seasoning

½ cup (67 g) frozen peas

½ cup (64 g) frozen carrots

2 cloves garlic, minced

1 tbsp (3 g) dried thyme

⅓ cup (41 g) all-purpose flour, plus more for dusting

1 cup (240 ml) chicken broth

2 cups (500 g) cooked, diced chicken

1 (12-oz [340-g]) package frozen puff pastry, 2 sheets, thawed according to the package directions

Heat the grill to medium-high heat.

Jump-start the potatoes by microwaving them. Pierce the potatoes all over with a fork and set them in a microwave-safe dish. Microwave at full power for 5 minutes. Use tongs to flip and cook for an additional 5 minutes. Continue to microwave in 1-minute intervals, as needed, until the potatoes are fork tender. Set aside to cool while you prep the filling mixture.

Melt the butter in a large skillet over medium-high heat. Add the chopped onion, season with a pinch of kosher salt and sauté until translucent, 10 to 12 minutes. Add the peas, carrots, garlic and thyme; again season with kosher salt and cook until fragrant, 1 to 2 minutes more. Sprinkle on the flour and cook for 2 minutes, or until the flour smells nutty and no longer looks dry. Add the chicken broth and stir, stir, stir until no lumps remain. Bring the pot pie mixture to a simmer and cook until it is thickened like gravy, about 10 minutes. Remove the pan from the heat, stir in the chopped chicken and set aside to cool. Be sure to taste this mixture and add more kosher salt, if needed, before filling the potato skins.

When the potatoes are cool enough to handle, cut them in half lengthwise, scoop out the tender potato insides (leave about ⅛-inch [3-mm] of potato in the skins for structure; you can save the potato innards for making Red Flannel Hipster Hash [page 161]) and set the potato skins on a rimmed baking dish. Spoon the pot pie mixture into the potato skins.

Unfold the puff pastry onto a lightly floured surface and use a large circle cutter to cut twelve rounds of puff pastry. Move the rounds to a parchment paper—lined baking sheet.

Cook the potato skins and puff pastry together on the grill. Bake until the puff pastry is golden brown and puffed, about 10 minutes, and the pot pie filling is bubbling. Top each potato skin with a puff pastry round just before serving.

EVERY SINGLE

GRILLED DESSERT RECIPE

You Will Ever Need to Know

We've grilled steak, chicken, pork, fish, veggies, sand-wiches and even cheese. Why would we stop at dessert? Sweets do well with a kiss of smoke and sugar that has caramelized on the grates of the grill. Don't fumble at the finish line, cook the dessert outside!

Grilled Donut ICE CREAM SANDWICHES

Serves: 4 to 6 | Prep Time: 10 minutes | Cook Time: 5 minutes

It's an ice cream sandwich. It's a donut. It's as fruity as pie. And it's the only grilled dessert recipe you will ever need to know. That's what our kids think anyway.

Oh, and the best part? The bits of the donut that touched the grill and turned into crunchy, sugary crystals were sent down to this earth from the heavens above.

3 cups (370 g) raspberries, divided

1 lemon, washed and dried

½ cup (100 g) sugar

Pinch of kosher salt

1 tbsp (8 g) cornstarch

1 tbsp (15 ml) water

6 glazed donuts

1 qt (544 g) vanilla ice cream

Sprinkles and chopped nuts, for serving

Heat the grill to medium. Set aside a few of the raspberries for garnish. Combine the rest of the raspberries with the zest and juice of the lemon, sugar and kosher salt in a saucepan, and bring to a simmer. Cook until the berries begin to burst, about 5 minutes. Whisk together the cornstarch and water, and slowly pour this into the sauce while stirring. As soon as the sauce starts to thicken, remove it from the heat to cool.

Slice the donuts in half, like a hamburger bun. Grill the donuts for 2 minutes on each side. Serve with a scoop of ice cream between the two donut halves, and roll in sprinkles or chopped nuts if you still feel like you need to be fucking fancy. Drizzle the whole beautiful mess with the raspberry sauce and garnish with the whole raspberries.

Acknowledgments

MARK'S ACKNOWLEDGMENTS

First and foremost, I'd like to acknowledge the love and support of my wife and creative partner in life, Sarah. The Grill Dads has taken me away from home for so much time over the years. And from the day I told her about the idea for doing The Grill Dads, to the day I told her we were going to do a TV show, to the day I told her we were doing this book, her response has always been, "you have to do it." And to my son, Arthur, who always welcomes me home with the biggest hug and so many ideas for what The Grill Dads should do next. I'd also like to thank my parents who have always supported my crazy endeavors, no matter how nervous they were about them.

I will forever love you Sarah, Arthur, Mom, Dad and Michele.

Additionally, I'd like to thank the amazing team at my company, UltraClean, for being my second family.

And to my partner in culinary crime, Ryan Fey, thanks for being a perfect partner. And a constant source of new material.

FEY'S ACKNOWLEDGMENTS

Wow. I can't believe they actually let us write a cookbook. See, Mom and Dad! I told you! :)

I am incredibly fortunate to have some of the best friends and family that support me in everything I do. Even though I sometimes question why . . . I love that they don't. First, I would like to acknowledge the incredible love and support that I get every single day from my daughter, Zoe. She is the most incredible kid and has always supported me when I have to dash out the door to catch a flight, wake up at the crack of dawn to cook and join countless meetings, and she's done it all with a smile and level of maturity that's well beyond her years. You rock, Zo!

To my parents, Dave and Cheryl, and my brother, Andy—what can I say, I'm the luckiest guy in the world to have such unparalleled love and support from you guys. You've always told me to go for it and to follow whatever path I choose. I love you so, so much.

And I'd like to thank my friends and family: Jonah, Sophie, Jeff, Dana, Eily, Chad, Scott, Freddie, Lachlan, Addy, Kiera, Julianna, Aunt Sherry, Gary, Helene and last but not least, Christy—I love you guys. To Zoe's mom, Amy—thank you so much for understanding my need to go through this journey and not wanting to kill me that much.

And last, to Mark—thank you for putting up with me. We're only just beginning.

THE GRILL DADS' ACKNOWLEDGMENTS

We've been lucky from the beginning of this adventure, starting all the way back when we put our show idea up on a crowdfunding site. A special thanks to Guy Fieri and Marc Summers for laughing at our dumb jokes, helping us get ready for a career in the culinary world and getting us on the Food Network. Thank you to Tom Mazzarelli and the entire crew at *The Today Show* for believing in us and letting us be a part of the show. Thanks to Jason, Gary, John, Rahsaan, Steve and the team at Howard Stern that bring us on the *Wrap-Up Show*. Thanks to Wendy Williams and her amazing team. Thanks to Max and J.B. for taking us back even though we made a dumb choice. Thanks to Trent and Fisco for helping us make great content. Thanks to Jeanne, Chip and all of our partners at Spiceology. Thanks to Amy Wilk for creative direction!

Thanks to Franny, Will and the team at Page Street Publishing for having a momentary lapse in judgment and allowing us to make this book. And for allowing us to be us. Thanks to Ken for taking such amazing pictures that made our food look so damn tasty, and to Amanda Hood for making the dishes look like a million bucks.

And finally, to the great Meghan Splawn. With zero exaggeration, we would have never taken this project on without knowing that you were willing to be a part of the team. Your guidance, leadership, culinary prowess, creative input and ability to put up with our shit is unmatched. We hope you're proud of this. We sure are.

A very special thank you to all the great partners and sponsors that have supported us, including Big Green Egg, Brixton®, Made In, Meater and Igloo®. Thank you to the incredible Eva for doing our Foreword.

About the Authors

Mark and Fey are real-life best buds, dad-joke enthusiasts and food fanatics that have found a home as entertainers on television and social media, and as a featured act at events.

They started their entertainment journey on the Food Network, as winners of Guy Fieri's *Guy's Big Project* and hosts of two primetime shows: *The Grill Dads* and *Comfort Food Tour*.

Before they were The Grill Dads, Fey spent his career as a creative and C-suite executive in advertising and was the co-founder of an award-winning creative advertising agency in Los Angeles. Mark was a C-suite advertising executive, small business owner and recovering tour manager for major international musicians, including Maroon 5 and Jennifer Hudson.

Mark and Fey believe in the unifying power of food to bring people together. They hope The Grill Dads' brand will invite everyone to the table to enjoy and create delicious meals to share with friends and family . . . because if they can do it, you can do it. Great food can happen right in your backyard, no culinary degree required.

Index